DYNAMIC PROGRAMMING
— FOR —
CODING
INTERVIEWS

All the programs in this book are compiled on GCC 4.9.2 compiler on Windows-10 machine with C99 mode enabled. If you still find error in the code or other text, or if you have any suggestion, feedbacks or any other comments, please send email to:

hikrawat@gmail.com

meenakshighangas@gmail.com

DYNAMIC PROGRAMMING

— FOR —

CODING INTERVIEWS

A Bottom-Up approach to problem solving

MEENAKSHI & KAMAL RAWAT

FOUNDER, RITAMBHARA TECHNOLOGIES

Notion Press

Old No. 38, New No. 6
McNichols Road, Chetpet
Chennai - 600 031

First Published by Notion Press 2017
Copyright © Meenakshi & Kamal Rawat 2017
All Rights Reserved.

ISBN 978-1-946556-69-1

DEDICATION

This book is dedicated to a yogi

MASTER MAHA SINGH

who mended relations and excelled in each role he lived

SON | BROTHER | FRIEND | HUSBAND | FATHER |
FATHER-IN-LAW | TEACHER | FARMER | CITIZEN |
DEVOTEE

the most upright, conscientious, and able man.

We miss you in every possible way Papa.

Contents

Preface

We have been teaching students 'How to prepare for Coding Interviews' for many years now.

A Data Structure problem like reverse a linked list or add operation `getMinimum()` to a Stack or implement a thread safe Queue are relatively easy to solve, because there are theoretical reference to start in such problems. The most difficult category of problems asked in coding competitions or interview of companies like Google, Amazon, Facebook, Microsoft etc. fall under the umbrella of Dynamic Programming (DP).

Most DP problems do not require understanding of complex data structure or programming design, they just need right strategy and methodical approach.

A solution is first visualized in the mind before it takes formal shape of an Algorithm that finally translates into a computer program. DP problems are not easy to visualize and hence not easy to solve.

The best way to visualize a DP problem is using recursion because DP problems demonstrates optimal substructure behavior. Recursion gives the right solution but usually takes exponential time. This unreasonably high time is taken because it solves subproblems multiple times.

DP is a bottom-up approach to problem solving where one subproblem is solved only once. In most cases this approach is counter-intuitive. It may require a change in the way we approach a problem. Even experienced coders struggle to solve DP problems.

This book is written with an intention that if a teacher reads it, he will make dynamic programming very interesting to his students. If this book is in the hands of a developer, he will feel super confident in answering algorithm questions in interviews, and anyone who read it will get a robust tool to approach problems asked in coding competitions.

Being a good coder is not about learning programming languages, it is about mastering the art of problem solving.

Code in this book is written in C language, If you have never written any program in C language, then we suggest you to read first few chapters of C from any good book and try writing some basic programs in C language.

Acknowledgments

To write a book, one need to be in a certain state of mind where one is secure inside himself so that he can work with single minded focus.

A guru helps you be in that state. We want to thank our ideological guru, Shri Rajiv Dixit Ji and Swamy Ramdev Ji.

The time spent on this book was stolen from the time of family and friends. Wish to thank them, for they never logged an FIR of their stolen time.

We also wish to thank each other, but that would be tantamount to one half of the body thanking the other half for supporting it. The body does not function that way.

How to Read this Book

We have discussed only simple problems in first six chapters. The idea is to explain concepts and not let the reader lost in complexity of questions. More questions are discussed in last three chapters with last chapter completely dedicated to practice questions.

If you have the luxury of time, then we strongly recommend you to read this book from cover to cover.

If you do not have time, then, how you read this book depends on how good you are in coding and how comfortable you are with recursion.

If you are good at forming logic and can write reasonably complex programs of Binary Tree and Linked List comfortably, then you may choose to skip the first chapter. I think the below logic may help you find a starting point

```
IF (one day left for Interview)
    IF (champion of DP)
        READ Chapter 8,9
    ELSE IF (Good @ Programming)
        READ Chapter 3, 4, 5, 6, 7.
    ELSE
        Pray to God, Start from Chapter 1.
ELSE IF (more than one week left for interview)
    IF (champion of DP)
        READ Chapter 2, 7, 8, 9
    ELSE IF (Student OR Researcher)
        READ complete book
ELSE IF (Reading to learn DP)
    READ complete Book
```

1

Recursion

```
int main() {
printf("Cannot stop till I die");
main();
}
```

Most computer concepts have their origin in Mathematics, Recursion is no exception. If you have studied mathematics at high school level, then you must have come across equations like.

$$\sum(n) = \begin{cases} n + \sum(n-1) & \text{, if } n>1 \\ 1 & \text{, if } n=1 \end{cases}$$

OR

$$Sum(n) = \begin{cases} n + Sum(n-1) & \text{, if } n>1 \\ 1 & \text{, if } n=1 \end{cases}$$

Σ is a symbol for summation. It is read as *"**Sum** of first **n** numbers is equal to **n** plus **Sum** of first (**n-1**) numbers. When **n** becomes 1, **Sum(1)** has a fixed value, 1." **n,** in this case is positive integer.

In plain words, Sum is defined in terms of Sum itself. This is called Recursion.

In computer programming, *"when a function calls itself either directly or indirectly it is called a Recursive Function and the process is called Recursion."*

Typically the function performs some part of the task and rest is delegated to the recursive call of the same function, hence, there are multiple instances of same function each performing some part of the overall task. Function stops calling itself when a terminating condition is reached.

> Recursion is a problem solving technique, where solution of a larger problem is defined in terms of smaller instances of itself.

Points to note in recursion are the following:

1. Recursion always have a **terminating condition** (else it will be infinite recursion). In Sum function, the condition, if n=1, then, stop recursion and return 1, is the terminating condition.

2. Recursive function **performs some part of task and delegate rest of it** to the recursive call. In above example, the function performs addition of n with the return value of the Sum(n-1) but delegate the computation of Sum(n-1) to recursive call.

Writing recursive code is not as difficult as it may appear, in fact, in most cases it is relatively simpler because we are not solving the complete problem. Recursive function code is a two-step process

1. Visualize the recursion by defining larger solution in terms of smaller solutions of the exact same type (with narrow parameters), and,

2. Add a terminating condition.

Example 1.1 translate the logic of calculating sum of first n positive integers to C language program.

Example 1.1: C language function to compute sum of first n positive numbers:

```
int sum(unsigned int n){
  if(n == 1)
    return 1;
  else
    return n + sum(n-1);
}
```

Code: 1.1

This code has an issue, If someone call it for n=0, then it will behave in an undefined manner.

As a good coding practice, we must check our program against boundary values of input parameters. If we call the function as
sum(0);

then, it will skip our terminating condition (n == 1) and enter into the recursion calling itself for n = -1, and this will make the result undefined[1].

We should be able to catch this issue while self-reviewing our code and should be able to correct it:

```
int sum(unsigned int n){
   // First terminating condition
   if(n == 0)
      return 0;

   // Second terminating condition
   if(n == 1)
      return 1;

   return n + sum(n-1);
}
```

Code: 1.2

We have just skipped the else part, because we are returning from the terminating conditions.

Code 1.2 may be written in a more compact form as shown below

```
int sum(int n){
   return (n==0)? 0: ((n==1)? 1: (n+sum(n-1)));
}
```

Code: 1.3

Which of the two codes should we prefer to write?

---

[1] In C language, conversion from signed to unsigned is not defined for negative numbers. For example, the value of y in the below code is not defined:

```
int x = -1;
unsigned int y = x;
```
When Sum is called for n=0. Then, it will skip the terminating condition and call the function recursively for n = -1.

Some coders, have an undue bias in favour of writing compact codes, this is especially true during the interview. Either they think that such code impress the interviewer, or they may just be in the habit of writing such code. Thumb rule for good code is,

"when there is a choice between simple and obfuscated code, go for the simpler one, unless the other has performance or memory advantage."

This rule is not just for interview, its generic. The code that we write is read by many people in the team, the simpler it is the better it is. One extra advantage of writing simple code during the interview is that, it provide us some space to correct mistakes there itself, because it leaves more white space on the paper.

The rule is just for spacing of code and choosing between two statements doing exactly same work. In no way a check should be omitted in favor of simplicity or clarity or extra space on the paper.

Never miss the terminating condition, else the function may fall into infinite recursion.

It is not mandatory to write a recursive function to compute sum of n numbers. It can be done using a loop without making any recursive call, as demonstrated in Code 1.4

Non-recursive code to compute sum of first n numbers

```
int sum(int n){
    int sum = 0;
    for(int i=1; i<=n; i++)
        sum += i;
    return sum;
}
```

Code: 1.4

Question 1.1: Factorial function is defined recursively for all non-negative integers as:

```
Fact(n) = n * Fact(n-1)    if n>1
        = 1                if n=1
```

Write both recursive and non-recursive function that accepts an unsigned int n and return factorial of n^2.

---

[2] Example7.1 in Chapter 7 gives the solution to this question.

Question 1.2: Given an array, `arr`, of integers, write a recursive function that add sum of all the previous numbers to each index of the array. For example, if input array is

1	2	3	4	5	6

Then, your function should update the array to

1	3	6	10	15	21

Example 1.2: Recursion to compute n^{th} power of a number x^n is defined as below:

$$x^n = \begin{cases} x * x^{n-1} & \text{, if } n>0 \\ 1 & \text{, if } n=0 \end{cases}$$

Function for above recursion is:

```
int power(int x, int n){
  if(0 == n)
     return 1;
  else if (1 == x)
     return x;
  else
     return x * power(x, n-1);
}
```

Code: 1.5

Recursive function in Code 1.5 accept two parameters. One of them remains fixed, and other changes and terminates the recursion. Terminating condition for this recursion is defined as

IF (n **EQUALS** 0) **THEN** return 1

But we have used two terminating conditions,

IF (n **EQUALS** 0) **THEN** return 1
IF (x **EQUALS** 1) **THEN** return x

This is to avoid unnecessary function calls when x is 1. In next chapter we will learn that every function call is an overhead, both in terms of time and memory.

The four things that we should focus on while writing a function (in this order) are:

1. It should serve the purpose. For every possible parameter the function must always return expected results. It should not be ambiguous for any input.

2. The time taken by function to execute should be minimized.

3. The extra memory this function consumes should be minimized.

4. Function should be easy to understand. Ideally the code should be self-explanatory to an extent that it does not even require any documentation (comments).

At no point during coding or while in the interview do we really care about how many lines of codes does particular function runs into as long as length of code is justified (we are not writing duplicate piece of code).

In next chapter, we will learn that a recursive solution takes more time and more memory than the corresponding iterative (non-recursive) solution. In Example 1.1, both iterative and recursive solutions are equally easy to code[3]. In such situations we should always go for non-recursive solution.

 INTERVIEW TIP

If both recursive and non-recursive (iterative) solutions are equally easy and take almost equal time to code, then always write the iterative solution. It takes less time and less memory to execute.

The advantage of recursion is that, sometimes, a solution that otherwise is very complex to comprehend, can be very easily visualized recursively. We just need to solve the problem for base case and leave rest of the problem to be solved by recursion. Consider Example 1.3 below:

Example 1.3: Tower of Hanoi

Tower of Hanoi is a Mathematical Game. There are 3 pegs (Rods), Source, Destination and Extra marked as S, D and E respectively, and there are n discs, each of different size, which can be inserted into any of these three pegs.

---

[3] Recursion is just replacing a loop in the iterative solution.

All discs are initially inserted into Source peg in decreasing order (smallest at the top) as shown in Picture 1.1 (for n=4).

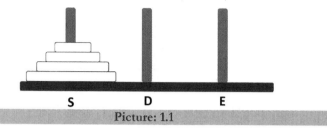

Picture: 1.1

We have to move all the discs from Source peg (S) to Destination peg (D). The final state should be as shown in Picture 1.2

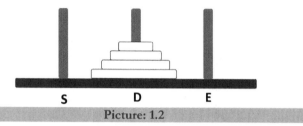

Picture: 1.2

There are 2 restrictions:

1. Only one disc can be moved at a time.
2. At any point in the process we should never place a larger disc on top of a smaller disc.

Write a function that accept characters representing three rods (S, D & E) and the number of discs (n), and print the movement of discs between pegs such that all discs are moved from the initial state (inside S) to the final state (inside D). Signature of the function is

```
/* s, d, e represents three pegs
 * (source, destination and extra).
 * n is number of discs (All initially in s)*/
void towerOfHanoi(char s, char d, char e, int n)
```

This may appear to be a complex problem to solve otherwise, but if we think recursively, then the problem can be solved in three simple steps

Step-1: Move n-1 discs from S to E using D

Let us assume that somehow n-1 discs are moved from S to E, and we have used D as the third peg (extra). This problem is similar to the original problem (of moving n discs from S to D using E).

After this step, the state of pegs and discs is as shown in the picture 1.3

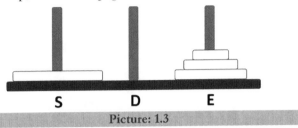

S   D   E

Picture: 1.3

Step-2: Move the n'th disc from S to D

Move Disc No. n from S to D. This is a single step of execution.

Step-3: Move n-1 discs from E to D using S

This problem is again of the same nature as step-1. Here we are moving n-1 discs from E to D using peg-S as extra.

If we carefully notice, Step-1 and Step-3, being problems of the same type, are recursive calls to the same function. Code 1.6 is the recursive function for Tower of Hanoi:

```
void towerOfHanoi(char s, char d, char e, int n){
  // TERMINATING CONDITION
  if(n <= 0)
    return;
  towerOfHanoi(s, e, d, n-1);
  printf("Move Disk-%d FROM %d TO %d", n, s, d);
  towerOfHanoi(e, d, s, n-1);
}
```

Code: 1.6

The terminating condition here is when there is no disk (n==0). Notice that we have put the condition as less-than or equal to, to handle cases when n is negative, alternatively, we can change signature of function to receive unsigned int in place of int.

If we call this function for 3 discs (n=3) like below

```
towerOfHanoi('s', 'd', 'e', 3);
```

8

The output is

```
Move Disk-1 FROM s TO d
Move Disk-2 FROM s TO e
Move Disk-1 FROM d TO e
Move Disk-3 FROM s TO d
Move Disk-1 FROM e TO s
Move Disk-2 FROM e TO d
Move Disk-1 FROM s TO d
```

Now we can appreciate, how helpful recursion can be even if it takes more time and more memory to execute.

Head Recursion and Tail Recursion

A Recursive function typically perform some task and call itself. If the call is made before the function performs its own task, then it is called Head-Recursion (*Recursion is performed at the head of the function body*). If recursive call is made at the end, then it is Tail-Recursion.

In Code 1.1, function sum(3), call function sum(2) first and then perform the add operation[4] (return value from sum(2) added with 3). This makes function sum, a head-recursive function.

To see the difference, consider Code 1.7 having two recursive functions to traverse a link list:

A recursive function is head-recursive if recursive call is made before it performs its own task. tail-recursion is when recursive call is made at end of the function (after it performs its own tasks).

```
/* Head Recursion.
 * First traverse rest of the list, then
 * print value at current Node. */
```

---

[4] **Tip:** In C language the order of e valuation of operands for plus operator (+) is not defined. It means that in the below statement:

```
x = fun1() + fun2();
```

x will be sum of return values of two functions but, whether fun1 is called first or fun2 is not defined in the language. This has to be defined by the compiler.

```
void traverse1(Node* head){
  if(head != NULL){
    traverse1(head->next);
    printf("%d", head->data);
  }
}

/* Tail Recursion.
 * First traverse rest of the list, then
 * print value at current Node. */
void traverse2(Node* head){
  if(head != NULL){
    printf("%d", head->data);
    traverse2(head->next);
  }
}
```

Code: 1.7

If below linked list is passed as input to the two functions in Code 1.7:

Then, `traverse1` function prints the list in backward order and `traverse2` prints it in forward order.

Output of traverse1: 4 3 2 1
Output of traverse2: 1 2 3 4

A tail recursion is very easy to re-write in form of a loop. So there should ideally be no reason to write a tail recursion in code unless we are writing it to demonstrate recursion itself.

Head and tail recursion are just given here as concepts. Most of the times (esp. in case of dynamic programming problems) recursion is more complex and may not be simple head or tail recursion. Consider one of the most rampant examples of recursion, in-order traversals of a Binary Tree.

In in-order traversal, we first traverse left subtree in in-order, then traverse (eg. print) the root and finally traverse the right subtree in in-order as shown in Picture 1.4.

Clearly the in-order function is defined in terms of in-order of left and right subtrees, hence recursion.

Algorithm:
1. Traverse Root
2. Traverse Left SubTree in PreOrder
3. Traverse Right SubTree in PreOrder

Output:
A B E C F G

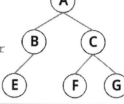

Picture: 1.4

If we take structure of the Node as below:

```
Struct Node{
  Node *left; // Pointer to Left subtree
  int data;
  Node *right; // Pointer to Right subtree
};
```

Then code of in-order traversal is as shown in Code 1.8 below:

```
/* Print In-Order traversal of the tree */
void inOrder(node* r){
  if(r == NULL)
    return;

  inOrder(r->left);
  printf("%d ", r->data);
  inOrder(r->right);
}
```

Code: 1.8

In the above code, recursion cannot be termed as either head or tail recursion.

The terminating condition that we have taken in Code 1.8 is when root is NULL. It will have extra function calls for leaf nodes, because function is called for left and right subtree even when both are NULL. A better solution is to check that a subtree is not NULL before calling the function for that subtree.

```
/* Print In-Order traversal of the tree */
void inOrder(node* r){
```

11

```
if(r == NULL)
  return;

if(r->left != NULL)
  inOrder(r->left);

printf("%d ", r->data);

if(r->right != NULL)
  inOrder(r->right);
}
```

Code: 1.9

It may look like small improvement, but it will reduce our number of function calls to almost half, because in a binary tree the number of null pointers is always greater than the number of valid pointers. In Code 1.8, we are making one function call for each pointer (null or non-null). But in code 1.9, the function calls are against non-null pointers only. Hence the total number of function calls in Code 1.9 is almost half as compared to function calls made in code 1.8.

Consider the below binary tree

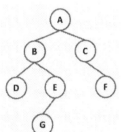

There are 8 null pointers, 6 as children of leaf nodes and right child of E and left child of C.

If we consider root also as one pointer (pointing to the root node, A), then total number of non-null pointers are 7 (one pointing to each node in the tree).

Putting such small checks not just optimize our code but also shows our commitment toward writing better code.

Next chapter discuss how does memory actually looks when a recursive function is called in contrast to an iterative function.

How to Solve a Problem Using Recursion

Our focus usually is to solve a problem, with recursion, we can actually code without solving a problem, if we can somehow define the large problem in terms of smaller problems of same type.

Our focus is on solving the problem for top case and leave the rest for recursive calls to do. Consider the below example:

Example 1.4: We all know about Bubble Sort, where an array is sorted in n passes as shown in the below code:

```
void bubbleSort(int *arr, int n)
{
  for(int i=0; i<n-1; i++)
    for(int j=0; j<n-i-1; j++)
      if(arr[j] > arr[j+1])
        swap(&arr[j], &arr[j+1]);
}
```

Code: 1.10

Where swap is a function that swaps two integers.

```
void swap(int *a, int *b){
  *a ^= *b;
  *b ^= *a;
  *a ^= *b;
}
```

Code: 1.11

Bubble Sort repeatedly steps through the array, compares each pair of adjacent items and swaps them if they are in the wrong order. After traversing for the first time, the largest element reaches last position in the array.

In the second pass, the second largest element reaches second last position and so on. There are n-1 passes that takes n-1 elements to their right positions, the nth element will be automatically at the first position.

Recursive implementation of Bubble Sort:

To make it a recursive function, we first need to define the larger problem in terms of smaller subproblems and task that each function will be performing. If the array is

9, 6, 2, 12, 11, 9, 3, 7

Then after the first pass, the largest element, 12, reach end of array:

6, 2, 9, 11, 9, 3, 7, **12**

With 12 at the nth position, we need to sort first n−1 elements. "*Sort first n elements*" and "*Sort first n-1 elements*" are same problems with different parameters. We have found our recursion, each function performs one pass and rest is left to recursion:

```
void bubbleSortRec(int *arr, int n){
  // Perform one pass
  for(int j=0; j<n-1; j++)
    if(arr[j] > arr[j+1])
      swap(&arr[j], &arr[j+1]);

  bubbleSortRec(arr, n-1);
}
```

Code: 1.12

We cannot be good coders without mastering the art of recursion. My suggestion to everyone reading this book is that when you write simple programs like linear search, binary search, sorting, etc. try to also implement them recursively. It will be a good net practice before the actual match.

Question 1.1: Below code print the mathematical table of n.

```
void printTable(int n){
  for(int i=1; i<=10; i++){
    printf("%d * %d = %d\n", n, i, (n*i));
  }
}
```

Code: 1.13

Write a recursive function that prints the mathematical table of n.

Hint: You may have to pass/accept i as parameter.

2

How it Looks in Memory

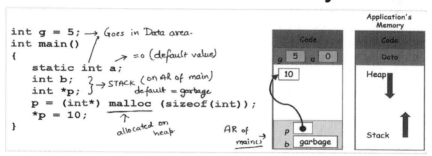

```
int g = 5; → Goes in Data area.
int main()
{                    → = 0 (default value)
    static int a;
    int b;  } → STACK (on AR of main)
    int *p; }       default = garbage
    p = (int*) malloc (sizeof(int));
    *p = 10;      ↑
}          allocated on
           heap
```

Before discussing how a recursive calls looks inside memory, we should understand how memory is divided internally and what part of the program goes in which section of the memory. This chapter is specific to C language, but the concepts are similar in other popular languages also.

Picture 2.1 shows lifecycle of a C language program:

Source Files ──╲
User-defined ──→ compile → Object File
Header Files ──╱

Linking ──→ Executable File

Standard ──╲
header files ──→ compile → Library File

Picture: 2.1

Read any good C language book to learn about compilation and linking of a C language program, this book assume that you have working knowledge of C language. After compiling and linking, [5] the binary executable of program gets generated (.exe on windows). When this executable binary is actually executing (running) it is called a **process**.

When a process is executed, first it is loaded into memory (RAM). Area of memory where process is loaded is called **process address space**. Picture 2.2 shows broad layout of process address space (*Picture 2.2 is independent of platform, actual layout may differ for operating system and for program*).

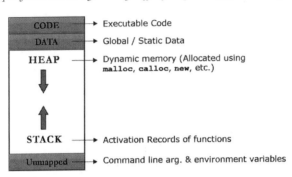

CODE	→ Executable Code
DATA	→ Global / Static Data
HEAP	→ Dynamic memory (Allocated using `malloc`, `calloc`, `new`, etc.)
STACK	→ Activation Records of functions
Unmapped	→ Command line arg. & environment variables

Picture: 2.2

This memory is allocated to our program by the operating system. The process address space has following segments

1. Code segment (or Text segment)
2. Data segment
3. Stack segment
4. Heap segment

In next section, we are discussing these segments one by one.

Code segment

✓ This segment contains machine code (in form of executable instructions) of the compiled program.

✓ It is read-only and cannot be changed when the program is executing.

✓ May be shareable so that only a single copy is in memory for different executing programs[6].

✓ Size of code segment is fixed at load time.

---

[5] Most IDEs compile, link and execute the program using a single button click. But internally all these steps are performed.

[6] Shareable code is outside the scope of this book.

Data Segment

✓ All global and static data variables are allocated memory in this segment.

✓ Memory is allocated in this area when the program is loading (before main function is called). That's why global and static variables are also called **load-time variables**.

✓ All load-time variables (global and static), are initialized at the load-time. If no initial value is given for a load-time variable then it is initialized with the zero of its type[7].

✓ Internally, this segment is divided in two areas, initialized and uninitialized. If initial value of a variable is given it goes in the initialized data area else it goes in the uninitialized data area. All the uninitialized variables are then initialized with zeros. The main reason why they are stored separately within data segment, is, bacause the uninitialized data area can be memset to zero in a single operation.

✓ Size of data segment is fixed at load time and does not change when program is executing.

Stack Segment

✓ Stack segment contains **Activation Records** (also called Stack Frames) of all the active functions. An active function is a function that is currently under the call. Consider Code 2.1 below

```
int main(){
    fun1();
}
void fun1(){
    fun2();
}
void fun2(){
}
void fun3(){
    // NEVER CALLED
}
```

Code: 2.1

---

[7] Zero of int data type is 0. Zero of pointer data type is NULL.

When main is called, it is the only active function. Then main calls fun1. At this point fun1 is executing but both main and fun1 are active. When fun1 calls fun2, then the execution is in fun2, but main, fun1 and fun2 are all active and has their activation records in Stack.

When function fun2 returns, then activation record of fun2 is poped from the Stack and execution is back in fun1. At this point main and fun1 are active and has their activation records in the Stack.

fun3, is never active, because it is never called and hence its activation record never gets created on the Stack.

✓ When a function is called, its Activation Record is created and pushed on the top of stack.

✓ When a function returns then the corresponding Activation Record is poped from the Stack.

✓ Size of Stack keeps changing while the program is executing because the number of active functions keep changing.

✓ Non-static local variables of a function are allocated memory inside Activation Record of that function when it is active.

✓ Variables that are allocated memory on Stack are not initialized by default. If initial value of a variable is not given then it is not initialized and its value will be garbage (this is different from load-time variables allocated memory in Data Segment).

✓ Activation record also contains other information required in function execution.

✓ Stack Pointer (SP register) keeps track of the top of the Stack.

✓ Point of execution is always inside the function whose activation record is on the top of Stack. Function whose activation record is inside Stack, but not at the top is active but not executing.

✓ If a function is recursive then multiple activation records of the function may be present on the Stack (one activation record for each instance of the function call).

Heap Segment

✓ When we allocate memory at run time using malloc(), calloc(), and realloc() in C language (new and new[] in C++), then that memory is allocated on the Heap. It is called **dynamic memory** or **run-time memory**.

✓ In C language we cannot initialize the memory allocated on Heap. In C++, if we use `new` operator to allocate memory, then we can initialize it using constructors.

✓ Memory allocated in heap does not have a name (unlike memory allocated in and Stack segments). The only way to access this memory is via pointers pointing to it. If we lose address of this memory, there is no way to access it and such a memory will become **memory leak**. It is one of the largest sources of error in C/C++ programming.

✓ Both Heap and Stack segment shares a common area and grows toward each other.

After compilation and linking, the executable code (in machine language) gets generated. The first thing that happens when this executable code is executed is that it is loaded in the memory. **Loading** has following steps:

✓ **Code goes in code area.** Code is in the form of binary machine language instructions and Instruction Pointer (IP register) holds the address of current instruction being executed.

✓ **Global and static variables are allocated memory in the data area**. Data area has two sub-parts, Initialized and Un Initialized data area, if initial value of a variable is given by us, it gets allocated in the initialized data area, else memory to the variable is allocated in the un-initialized data area and it is initialized with zero.

✓ **Global and static variables are initialized**. If we have given the initial value explicitly, then variables are initialized with that value otherwise they are initialized with zeros of their data types.
```
int x = 5; // initialized with 5
int y;     // initialized with 0
```

After these steps, we say that *the program is loaded*. After loading is complete, the `main` function is called[8] and actual execution of the program begins. Read the entire program given in Code 2.2 carefully:
```
// Go in data area at load time. Initialized with 0.
int total;

/** Code (machine instructions) of function goes in
 * code area. When this function is called, then
```

---

[8] **Question:** Who calls the main function ?

19

```
 * Activation Record of the function is created on
 * Stack.
 */
int square(int x){
   // x goes in AR⁹ when this function is called.
   return x*x;
}


/** Code of function goes in the code area. When this
 * function is called (at run-time), its AR gets
 * created on Stack and memory to non-static local
 * variables (x and y) is allocated in that AR.
 * count, being a static variable, is allocated in
 * data area at load time.
 */
int squareOfSum(int x, int y){
   static int count = 0; // Load-time var
   printf("Fun called %d times", ++count);
   return square(x+y);
}


/** Code goes in code area. When main is called, its
 * activation record gets created on Stack and memory
 * to non-static local variables (a and b) is
 * allocated in that Activation Record.
 */
int main(){
   int a=4, b=2;
   total = squareOfSum(a, b);
   printf("Square of Sum = %d",total);
}
```

Code: 2.2

This program computes $(a+b)^2$ and print the result. To keep it simple, we are using the hard coded values 4 and 2 for a and b respectively. The function squareOfSum also keeps a count of how many times it is called in a static variable count, and print the count every time it is called.

Code 2.2 may not be the best implementation, but it serves our purpose. Read the code again, especially the comments before each

---

[9] AR = Activation Record

20

function and make sure that we understand everything.

After compilation and linking, the executable of the program is created and when this executable is run, the first thing that happens is that this executable is loaded in the memory (RAM). At this point the `main` function is not yet called and the memory looks like Picture 2.3:

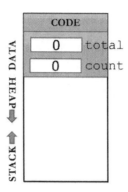

Picture: 2.3

After loading is complete, `main` function is called. When a function is called, its Activation Record is created and pushed in the Stack. The AR has

✓ Local (non-static) variables of a function (a and b for `main`).
✓ Other things stored in the Activation Record.

In the diagrams, we are only showing non-static local variables in Activation Records. After `main` function is called, the memory looks as shown in Picture 2.4

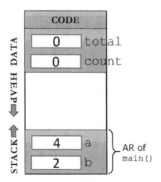

Picture: 2.4

At any time, the point of execution (Instruction Pointer) is in the function whose AR is at the top of Stack. Let us understand what all happens internally during a function call.

When a function is called:

1. State (register values, Instruction Pointer value, etc.) of calling function is saved[10] in the memory.

2. Activation record of called function is created and pushed on the top of Stack. Local variables of called function are allocated memory inside the AR.

3. Instruction pointer (IP register) moves to the first executable instruction of called function.

4. Execution of the called function begins.

Similarly when the called function returns back (to the calling function), following work is done:

1. Return value of the function is stored in some register.

2. AR of called function is popped from the memory (Stack size is reduced and freed memory gets added to the free pool, which can be used by either the stack or heap).

3. State of the calling function is restored back to what it was before the function call (Point-1 in function call process above).

4. Instruction pointer moves back to the instruction where it was before calling the function and execution of calling function begins from the point at which it was paused[11].

5. Value returned from called function is replaced at the point of call in calling function.

---

[10] Value of local variables of a function under execution are stored in the AR of function which is preserved in the stack. But Registers will also have some values, these values also need to be saved (because Registers are needed by the called function). This state is saved in the memory.

[11] This is conceptually similar to **Context Switch** of process contexts in a muti-processing operating system when one process is preempted to execute another process and after some time control returns back to the first process and it starts executing from the same point where it was preempted.

> Clearly, a function call is a lot of overhead both in terms of time and memory.

One of the reasons behind the popularity of macros in C language (even after all the evil that they bring along) is this overhead in function call. Another was the type independence that macros bring[12].

Some compilers optimize the performance by replacing function call with entire code of the function during compilation, hence avoiding the actual function call overheads. This is called inline expansion. For example, in Code 2.2, the compiler may just put entire code of function `square` inside `squareOfSum` and remove the function call all together as shown below.

```
int squareOfSum(int x, int y){
    static int count = 0; // Load-time var
    printf("Fun called %d times", ++count);
    return (x+y) * (x+y);
}
```

Code: 2.3

Recursive functions are very difficult to expand inline because compiler may not know the depth of function call at compile time.

Example 2.1: Let us also see how memory looks like if we miss the terminating condition in recursion. Code 2.4 is example of infinite recursion.

```
int main(){
    int x = 0;
    x++;
    if(x<5){
        printf("Hello");
        main();
    }
}
```

Code: 2.4

When the program is executed after compilation, it is first loaded in the memory and then the `main` function is called. At this point (after

---

[12] In C++, both the benefits are given in the form of inline functions and templates and they are not error prone like macros.

23

calling `main`) the memory looks as shown in Picture 2.5. Code area has the code, The Data area is empty because there is no load-time (global or static) variable. Stack has only one activation record of function `main`.

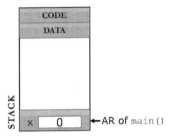

Picture: 2.5

Initial value of x is 0, after increment x become 1, since x<5, the condition is true and `main` is called again. A new AR for this newly called `main` is created on the Stack and this AR also has local variable x that is different from variable x in AR of previous call (see Picture 2.6). Value of this new x is again 0, and `main` is called again. Every time `main` is called, the value of x in the new activation record is 0.

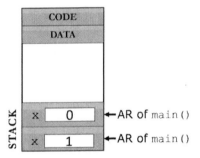

Picture: 2.6

Every instance of `main` is actually using a different x (from their own instance of AR).

Code 2.4 will continue to print "Hello", until a point when no space is left in the Stack to create new AR. At this point `main` cannot be called further and the program will crash.

An important thing to note is that the program will not print "Hello" infinitely. It is printed, till the memory stack overflows.

24

Recursive v/s Non-Recursive Inside Memory

Let us consider Example 1.1 from chapter-1 again.

```
int sum(int n){
  if(n==1)
    return 1;
  else
    return n + sum(n-1);
}
```

Code: 2.5

When we call this function for n=3, as sum(3); It will call sum(2); which will in-turn call sum(1);

At this point (when execution control is in sum(1)), the memory stack will have three instances of activation records of function sum, each having a local variable n, as shown in Picture 2.7.

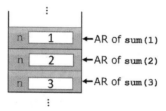

Picture: 2.7

In the iterative version (Code 1.4) there is only one function call to sum(3) and three local variables n, i and sum on the Activation Record (AR) of the function as shown in Picture 2.8.

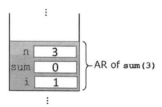

Picture: 2.8

In recursive version, one activation record is created for each value of n. If n=1000 then 1000 ARs are created. Therefore the extra memory taken is O(n). Table 2.1 gives a comparison of asymptotic running time and extra memory taken for recursive and non-recursive sum functions.

The asymptotic time may be same, O(n) for both the cases, but actual time taken for recursive version is much more than the iterative version because of the constant multiplier.

	Recursive	Non-Recursive
Time	O(n)	O(n)
Memory	O(n)	O(1)

Table: 2.1

Example 2.2: Let us consider one more example. Code 2.6 is the recursive function to computes factorial of n:

```
int factorial(int n){
    if(1==n || 0==n)
        return 1;
    else
        return n * factorial(n-1);
}
```

Code: 2.6

If function is called for n=4,

```
fact(4);
```

from some other function to compute factorial of 4. During successive function calls, the memory looks like Picture 2.9.

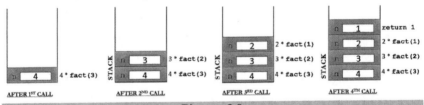

Picture: 2.9

When the functions return value to their caller functions, the AR will be poped from the stack and the stack will look like Picture 2.10 (return values shown on right side).

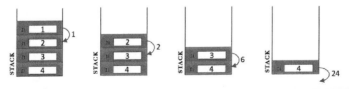

Picture: 2.10

There will also be other function's AR in the Stack (eg. `main` function). They are not shown to save the space.

Code 2.7 shows the non-recursive code to compute factorial of n.

```
int factorial(int n){
  int f = 1;
  for(int i=2; i<=n; i++)
    f = f * i;
  return f;
}
```

Code: 2.7

The memory image of function in Code 2.7 is shown in Picture 2.11. Compare it with the memory taken by the recursive code.

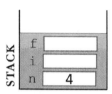

Picture: 2.11

Code 2.7 may have more local variables, but there is just one AR in the memory irrespective of the value of n.

Recursion is a huge overhead. Both in terms of memory and execution time.

The examples of recursion seen till now are simple linear recursions. One of the major problem with recursive function comes when recursive calls starts overlapping at the level of subproblems. Overlapping subproblems is discussed in detail in chapter 4.

Memory Layout as a Problem-Solving Tool

A clear understanding of lifecycle of program execution and how a program is loaded in memory comes handy in solving many more questions other than recursion. Consider the below examples:

Example 2.3: What is value of x in the below code?

```
static int x = strlen("Hello");
```

The above code is compile-time error. To put it simply, *"static and global variables cannot be initialized with the return value of a function."*

We are trying to initialize a static variable with the return value of function `strlen`.

We know that static variables are initialized at load time.

But wait, functions cannot be called at load time. A function can only be called when loading is complete and the program is executing (first function that gets called is `main`).

How can we initialize, at load-time, with something that is not available until execution time. Hence, Error!

What if we break up the statement in two parts?

```
static int x;         // Initialized with zero
x = strlen("Hello");
```

Now there is no problem. At load time variable x is **initialized** with zero. During execution the function `strlen("Hello")` is called and x is **assigned** the value 5.

Example 2.4: What value will get printed if we call function `fun`?

```
void fun(){
    int a = 5;
    static int b = a;
    printf("Value: %d", b);
}
```

Code: 2.8

No, the answer is not 5 or 0. The above code is also a compile time ERROR.

We know, static variables are initialized at load time. In code 2.8 we are initializing b with a, but variable a, is not available while loading. It will be allocated memory in the activation record when function `fun` is called and `fun` is called at execution-time. It is called only after the loading is complete and when the code starts executing.

Also, if there are more than one instances of any function in the Stack (in case of recursive functions). Then each AR have a separate copy of local variable `a`, but there is only one copy of static variable (allocated in the data area). By that logic also static variable (single copy) cannot be initialized with a local variable (possible zero or multiple copies).

Load-time variables cannot be initialized with local variables.

Conclusion

1. A function will have multiple ARs inside stack **if and only if** it is recursive.

2. Global and static variables can only be initialized with constants.

3. The memory to load-time variables is allocated before any function is called.

4. The memory to load-time variables is released only after the execution is complete.

We have not discussed the Heap area because the purpose was to explain recursion and not pointers or dynamic memory allocation or deallocation. To learn how heap area is used, read some good book on pointers in C language.

3

Optimal Substructure

Optimal substructure means, that optimal solution to a problem of size n (having n elements) is based on an optimal solution to the same problem of smaller size (less than n elements). i.e while building the solution for a problem of size n, define it in terms of similar problems of smaller size, say, k (k < n). We find optimal solutions of less elements and combine the solutions to get final result.

Example 3.1: Consider finding the shortest path for travelling between two cities by car. A person want to drive from city A to city C, city B lies in between the two cities.

There are three different paths connecting A to B and three paths connecting B to city C as shown in Picture 3.1:

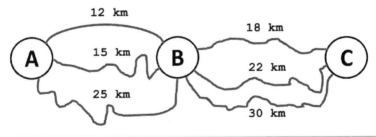

12 km

18 km

15 km

22 km

25 km

30 km

Picture: 3.1

The shortest path of going from A to C (30 km) will involve both, taking the shortest path from A to B and shortest path from B to C. It means:

1. If the shortest route from Delhi to Mumbai passes thru Pathmeda, then it will be the sum of shortest route from Delhi to Pathmeda and shortest route from Pathmeda to Mumbai.

2. If the shortest route from Delhi to Mumbai passes thru Jaipur and Pathmeda then the shortest route from Jaipur to Mumbai also passes thru Pathmeda.

In other words, the problem of getting from Delhi to Pathmeda is nested within the problem of getting from Delhi to Mumbai.

In a nutshell, it means, we can write recursive formula for a solution to the problem of finding shortest path.

We say, that the problem of finding the shortest route between two cities demonstrates optimal substructure property. This is one of the two conditions of dynamic programming. Another condition is overlapping subproblems, discussed in Chapter-4.

Standard algorithms like Floyd–Warshall and Bellman–Ford to find all-pair shortest paths are typical examples of Dynamic Programming.

Example 3.2: Consider now, the problem to find the longest path between two cities. Given four cities, A, B, C and D. The distance between them is as shown in Picture 3.2:

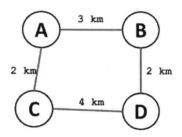

Picture: 3.2

The longest distance from A to D is 6 km, via city C. But this path is not the combination of longest path from A to C and C to D because the longest path between A and C is 9 km (via B and D).

31

Clearly longest path problem does not have the optimal substructure property (and hence not a DP problem).

Use of Optimal Substructure in DP

Fundamentally, DP is an important tool for optimizing recursive solutions in a way that is more efficient, both in terms of memory and time than regular recursion.

Writing a recursive formula or defining the optimal substructure is the first step toward dynamic programming. If we cannot write a recursive formula for the problem, we may not be thinking about using dynamic programming.

The logic of dynamic programming usually comes from recursion. Solution of a problem is derived from solution of subproblems, solution of subproblem is derived from solution of sub-subproblems and so on.

In questions of dynamic programming, it is a good idea, to first solve the problem using recursive formula and then use the same formula with bottom-up approach of dynamic programming.

Next chapter discuss the second property of dynamic programming, overlapping subproblems and in successive chapters we discuss two more problem solving approaches, Memoization and bottom-up dynamic programming.

4

Overlapping Subproblems

```
The book delayed because of laziness, procrastination and
             lack of discipline. Oops! The problems overlap.
```

All the recursive problems we discussed in previous chapters were singular in nature. We were using recursion, but each subproblem was solved only once.

In this chapter we focus on complex recursions. Recursive function is called with exactly same parameters more than once. In this case we say that a subproblem is solved multiple times.

Example 4.1: Consider the example of finding n^{th} term of Fibonacci series[13]. Below is the Fibonacci series
```
1, 1, 2, 3, 5, 8, 13, 21, ...
```

First two terms are both 1, and each subsequent term is sum of previous two terms. Recursive definition of Fibonacci number is
```
Fibonacci(1) = Fibonacci(2) = 1              if n = 1,2
Fibonacci(n) = Fibonacci(n-1)+Fibonacci(n-2)  for n>2
```

---

[13] Fibonacci sequence appears in Indian mathematics, in connection with Sanskrit prosody dated back to 450 B.C. Like most other things, the series went from east to west and was named after the guy who introduced it to west, rather than the original founders, that guy happens to be Fibonacci.

The simplest algorithm to compute n^{th} term of Fibonacci is direct translation of mathematical definition:

```
int fib(int n){
   if (n==1 || n==2)
      return 1;
   else
      return fib(n-1) + fib(n-2);
}
```

Code: 4.1

Code 4.1 is a recursive code. We may want to put an extra check and throw an exception if n is negative or zero, so that our code does not run into infinite recursion if called with zero or negative value as argument. We skipped this check to keep the code simple.

It may not be obvious, but Example 4.1 also has optimal substructure property. To find optimal solution (the only solution in this case) for n^{th} term we need to find the optimal solution for $n-1^{th}$ term and $n-2^{th}$ term.

The equation of time taken by the function in Code 4.1 is

```
T(n)  =  T(n-1)  +  T(n-2)  +  O(1)
```

This is an equation for exponential time. The reason why it is taking exponential time for such a simple algorithm is because it is solving the subproblems (computing k^{th} term, $k<n$) multiple times. Picture 1.1 show function calls for n=5, each node in the picture represents a function call and value in the node represents value of n in that call.

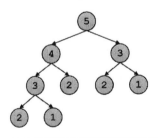

Picture: 4.1

The function `fib(n)`, where n=5, call itself twice with n=4 and n=3. Function with n=4 will in turn call `fib` function twice with n=3 and n=2. Note that `fib(3)` is called twice, from `fib(4)` and `fib(5)` respectively (see Picture 4.2). In fact `fib(2)` is called three times.

In all the examples of recursion seen in first three chapters, each subproblems was solved only once. But, when we compute 20th term of Fibonacci using Code 4.1 (call `fib(20)`), then `fib(3)` is called 2584 times and `fib(10)` is called 89 times. It means that we are computing the 10th term of Fibonacci 89 times **from scratch**.

In the ideal world, if we have already computed value of `fib(10)` once, we should not be recomputing it again. Had we been computing one term only once (solving a subproblem only once), the code would have been really fast, even if we are using recursion. Memoization, Dynamic programming and Greedy approach are techniques used to solve this classic problem.

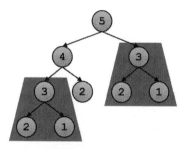

Picture: 4.2

Code 4.2 has non-recursive function to find the nth term of Fibonacci. First and second terms are both 1. Third term is computed using the first two, then we compute the 4th term using this 3rd term and 2nd terms and move forward like this till we reach the nth term as shown in Code 4.2.

```
int fib(int n){
    int a = 1, b = 1, c, cnt = 3;
    if(n == 1 || n ==2)
        return 1;
    for (cnt = 3; cnt <= n; cnt++)
    {
        c = a + b;
        a = b;
        b = c;
    }
    return c;
}
```

Code: 4.2

Code 4.2 is taking `O(n)` time and constant extra memory. Table 4.1 gives a comparison of number of times function `fib` is called for different values of n for recursive and iterative version:

n =	2	3	4	5	10	20	40
Recursive	1	3	5	9	109	13529	204668309
Iterative	1	1	1	1	1	1	1

Table: 4.1

Above table is a comparison of number of function calls made. But the time taken by recursive and non-recursive functions are not same. One instance of recursive function is taking `O(1)` time, in non-recursive the function instance is taking `O(n)`. But there will always be only one instance of function called irrespective of the value of n.

When we called the functions for n=20, then the recursive function in Code 4.1 took `65.218` time where as non-recursive code in Code 4.2 took `0.109` time (time in micro seconds measured on a slow machine).

To understand it better, non-recursive code will take about one second to compute the same term for which recursive code will take more than 10 minutes. And this is for relatively smaller value of n, when function is called for n=80 (i.e `fib(80)`), the recursive code took hours and non-recursive code does not take even a second.

It is difficult to believe that such an innocent looking code can hang our system for as small a value of n as `80`. The culprit is overlapping subproblems. Example 4.2, discuss one more example of overlapping subproblems:

Example 4.2: There are N stations in a route, starting from 0 to N-1. A train moves from first station (0) to last station (N-1) in only forward direction. The cost of ticket between any two stations is given, Find the minimum cost of travel from station 0 to station N-1.

Solution:

First we have to define for ourselves, the data structure in which cost of ticket between stations is stored. Let us assume that there are four stations (0 to 3) and cost of ticket is stored in a 4*4 matrix, as below.

```
cost[4][4] = { { 0, 10, 75, 94},
               {-1,  0, 35, 50},
               {-1, -1,  0, 80},
               {-1, -1, -1,  0}
             };
```

36

`cost[i][j]` is cost of ticket from station `i` to station `j`. Since we are not moving backward, `cost[i][j]` does not make any sense when `i > j`, and hence they are all `-1`. If `i==j`, then we are at the same station where we want to go, therefore all the diagonal elements are zeros.

In fact this is a fit case to use sparse arrays[14].

 INTERVIEW TIP

Our solution in the interview may not be the most optimized in terms of time or memory, because the time available during the interview is limited. But as a candidate we should always talk about the scope of improvements in our code. For example, in the above solution, you may use 2-dim array but you should apprise the interviewer that using sparse arrays may be better in this case.

If we want to move from `station-0` to `station-2` then the cheapest way is to take the ticket of `station-1` from `station-0` and then again take the ticket of `station-2` from `station-1`. This way total cost of travel is Rs. 45 (10+35). If we take direct ticket of `station-2` from `station-0` then the cost of travel is Rs. 75.

In the given example there are 4 stations, and we need to compute minimum cost of travel from `station-0` to `station-3`.

If `minCost(s, d)` is minimum cost of traveling from `station-s` to `station-d`. The Minimum cost to reach `N-1` from `0` can be recursively defined as

```
minCost(0, N-1)
        = MIN { cost[0][n-1],
                cost[0][1] + minCost(1, N-1),
                minCost(0, 2) + minCost(2, N-1),
                ... ... ...,
                minCost(0, N-2) + cost[N-2][n-1] }
```

First option is to go directly to station `N-1` from `station-0` without

---

[14] A sparse array is simply an array most of whose entries are zero (or null, or some other default value). The occurrence of zero-value elements in a large array is inefficient for both computation and storage. So rather than keeping the array as it is (with empty cells), the non-empty cells are stored in some other data structure and empty cells are not stored at all.

any break. Second option is to break at station-1 and so on. When we break at station-i, we calculate the min cost of moving from 0 to i and then the min cost of moving from i to N-1. Note that we are not going to station N-1 directly from i, we are just ensuring a break at station-i.

There are two terminating conditions for above recursion as defined below:

```
// 1. When both station are same.
IF(s == d) return 0.
```

```
// 2. when s is just before d, then there is only
// one way to reach d from s.
IF(s == d-1) RETURN cost[s][d].
```

Both the above conditions can be merged into one (because cost[s][d] is also 0 when s == d).

```
IF (s == d || s == d-1) RETURN cost[s][d].
```

Implementation of this recursive solution is given in Code 4.3:

```
// Two dim array having cost of tickets.
int cost[N][N];

// Calculate min cost from source(s) to destination(d)
int calculateMinCost(int s, int d){

  if (s == d || s == d-1)
    return cost[s][d];

  int minCost = cost[s][d];
  // Try every intermediate station to find min
  for (int i = s+1; i<d; i++)
  {
    // MinCost of going from s to i.
    // and MinCost of going from i to d.
    int temp = calculateMinCost(s, i) +
               calculateMinCost(i, d);
    if (temp < minCost)
      minCost = temp;
```

```
    }
    return minCost;
}
```

To calculate the minimum cost for travelling from `station-0` to `N-1` call the above function as:

```
calculateMinCost(0, N-1);
```

Note that solution of Code 4.3 demonstrates **optimal substructure** property. Because we are computing the min cost of travel between intermediate stations to find the actual min cost of going from initial source to final destination.

The code is also solving a subproblem multiple times. For example, to find min cost from `station-0` to `station-4` we are computing min cost of `station-1` to `station-3` twice as shown in Picture 4.3.

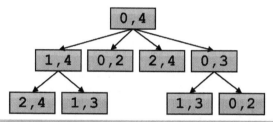

Picture: 4.3

If there are 10 stations, then we will be solving this subproblem of computing the min cost of travelling from `station-1` to `station-3`, 144 times. Just imagine, if we have 100 stations then how many times we are computing minimum cost to move from say, `station-10` to `station-20` as part of solving the main problem. Code 4.3 takes exponential time because of these overlapping subproblems.

 INTERVIEW TIP

A recursive exponential-time solution is usually an acceptable answer in the interview because even interviewer understand that the available time is limited.

It is good interview practice to put a quick not-so-optimized fully-working and bug-free solution on the table and then work on optimizing it, instead of getting stuck and not responding in the process of coming up with most the optimal solution.

First it will create an impression on the interviewer that you can handle unknown problems methodically and come to a quick solution, second it will comfort you that you have at least given one fool-proof working solution, so even if you are not able to give the best solution, it is still not that bad.

Also, you may not get time to execute all the steps during the interview. Going ahead with the quick recursive solution will go in your favor. Just make sure to handle the boundary condition properly in the implementation and leave no bug in the code.

Once you present that solution on the paper and tell the interviewer that, it can be optimized further if we use dynamic programming, Interviewer may take it on the face value and give you complete credit for optimized solution without even asking you for the solution. If there is time, the interviewer may ask you to optimize your solution.

Having said that, if you can come up with the optimized DP answer easily then you must go for it.

 ### CODING COMPETITION TIP

In a coding competition (Online or otherwise) the recursive solution may not be the way to go forward. In an online competition, you may find some of the test cases failing because of the high execution time taken by recursive code (even when the solution is right). Also, in the competition, your code will be checked against the code of other contestants.

Question 4.1: Given a matrix of order N*N. What are the total number of ways in which we can move from the top-left cell (`arr[0][0]`) to the bottom-right cell (`arr[N-1][N-1]`), given that we can only move either downward or rightward?

This problem is discussed in Example 9.2.

5

Memoization

I wish we could choose which memories to remember.

In the previous chapter we saw how recursive solution may be solving the same subproblem multiple times. It happens in case of overlapping subproblems and it may take time complexity of the code to exponential levels.

Recursion itself is bad in terms of execution time and memory. In Code 4.1, the problem gets worse when we compute value of fib(x) from scratch again even when it was computed earlier (overlapping subproblems).

When fib(10) is calculated for the first time we can just remember the result and store it a cache. Next time when a call is made for fib(10) we just look into the cache and return the stored result in O(1) time rather than making 109 recursive calls all over again. This approach is called **Memoization**.

In memoization we store the solution of a subproblems in some sort of a cache when it is solved for the first time. When the same subproblem is encountered again, then the problem is not solved from scratch, rather, it's already solved result is returned from the cache. Flow chart in Picture 5.1 shows the flow of execution pictorially:

Consider Code 4.1 again (computing n^{th} Fibonacci term), let us add an integer array, memo of size N that will act as cache to store result of subproblems (N = max value of n that need to be computed).

```
int memo[N] = {0};
```

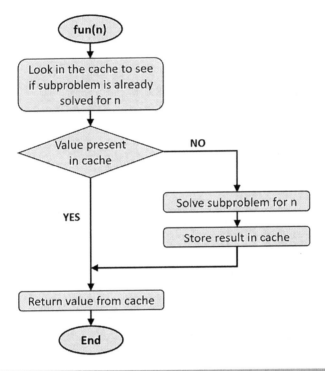

Picture: 5.1

All elements of array are initialized to zero. When k^th Fibonacci term is computed for the first time it is stored in memo[k]. When the function gets called again for n=k (to compute k^th Fibonacci term), we just return memo[k] in constant time rather than computing it again ($O(2^k)$ time operation). Code 5.1 is the memoized version of Code 4.1:

```
// This array will store fib(k) at k'th index.
// memo[k]==0 means fib(k) is not yet computed
int memo[N] = {0};

int fib(int n){
    //If fib(n) already computed, don't compute again
    if(memo[n] != 0)
        return memo[n];

    // compute fib(n) and store it at memo[n].
```

```
if(n==1 || n==2)
  memo[n] = 1;
else
  memo[n] = fib(n-1)+fib(n-2);

return memo[n];
}
```

Code: 5.1

Function fib(n) will call itself recursively only when it is called for the first time for n, in subsequent calls for the same value it will just do a look-up in the array.

There are two types of call to the function, one that does actual computation and hence may call itself recursively and other that just do a look-up in the array and return the already stored result. The former is non-memoized call and later ones are all memoized calls.

There will be exactly O(n) non-memoized calls and each call takes constant time, because if fib(4) and fib(3) are already computed then non-memoized call of fib(5) will add the two and take constant time. Total time taken to compute n^{th} term of Fibonacci is O(n). We have optimized an exponential time function to take linear time using a simple cache.

Let us extend Table 4.1, of previous chapter and add one more row in it:

n =	2	3	4	5	10	20	40
Recursive	1	3	5	9	109	13529	204668309
Iterative	1	1	1	1	1	1	1
Memo	1	3	5	7	17	37	77

Table: 5.1

For n=100, the function, fib(100), in Code 5.1 is called just 197 times. For the sake of comparison, if one function call takes one sec to execute[15]. Then Code 5.1 will take 1.28 minutes to compute 40th term.

---

[15] This is just an assumption. Actual machines runs much faster. A 2 GHz CPU (two gigahertz) goes through 2,000,000,000 cycles per second. One instruction may take one or more CPU cycles. Usually a O(1) function call will take time in microseconds.

Whereas recursive function in Code 4.1 will take 6.5 years to compute the same term. Thankfully we have faster computers that are overriding our bad code and are doing the work of years in seconds.

Example 4.2 of previous chapter is also solving subproblems multiple times. The recursive solution in Code 4.3 can also be memoized in a similar way. But in this case the cache cannot be a one-dimensional array because subproblems in this case has two parameters, s and d:

*Find minimum cost to travel from **Station-s** to **Station-d***

We take a two dimensional array of size N*N as cache to stores minimum cost of traveling between two stations.

```
int memo[N][N] = {0};
```

Once the minimum cost is computed for traveling from station-s to station-d, this value is stored in cell memo[s][d]. Next time when the function is called with same parameters (to compute min cost from station-s to station-d), we do not compute the min cost again and just return the value stored in memo[s][d] (constant time).

Deciding data structure of cache is important step in memoization. The cache should be capable of storing results of all subproblems. Usually cache is an array. If our problem has only one dimension, then it is one-dim array, else we use multi-dimensional array.

Memoized solution of Example 4.2 is shown in Code 5.2 below:

```
// Cache used for Memoization
int memo[N][N] = {0};

int calculateMinCost(int s, int d){
   if (s == d || s == d-1)
     return cost[s][d];

   // Enter only if value is not yet computed
   if(memo[s][d] == 0)
   {
     // Code Similar to recursive version
```

```
int minCost = cost[s][d];

for (int i = s+1; i<d; i++)
{
  // Cost of going from s to i directly
  // and then from i to d directly.
  int temp = calculateMinCost(s, i) +
             calculateMinCost(i,d);
  if (temp < minCost)
    minCost = temp;
}

// Store the minCost in cache
memo[s][d] = minCost;
}
return memo[s][d];
}
```

Code: 5.2

Code 5.2 takes $O(n^2)$ extra memory and $O(n^3)$ time. This is a huge improvement over the exponential time recursive solution in Code 4.3.

Memoization is Recursion

Memoization is a strong technique, it improves the performance in a big way by avoiding multiple re-computations of subproblems. The goodness of recursion (to be able to visualize a problem and solve it in a top-down fashion) is used without the side effects of overlapping subproblems that comes with recursion.

Memoization = Recursion
             + Cache
               – Recomputing overlapping subproblems

From Chapter 2 we know that even without overlapping subproblems recursion itself is an overhead because multiple instances of Activation Record gets created in the stack (and each AR creation and removal is a cost in terms of both memory and time). Memoization uses recursion, do I need to say more about room for improvements in memoization.

In fact, if there are no overlapping subproblems then memoization will be exactly similar to recursion in terms of execution time.

The dynamic programming approach discussed in next chapter is the bottom-up approach to problem solving that reduces both time and space complexity further.

6

Dynamic Programming

Energy of a nation is like sap of a tree,
it rises bottom-up.

Before moving further, let us understand that the way Apple Inc. is not related to 'Apple' the fruit in any way, Dynamic programming has nothing to do with being dynamic or even programming. It is just an approach to problem solving.

Wikipedia defines Dynamic programming as *"A method for solving a complex problem by breaking it down into a collection of simpler subproblems, solving each of those subproblems just once, and storing their solutions - ideally, using a memory-based data structure."*

By this definition, memoization is also dynamic programming. Some authors in fact use the term *"Memoized Dynamic Programming"* or *'Top-Down dynamic programming'* for Memoization and they use *"Bottom-up dynamic programming"* to describe what we are calling Dynamic Programming here.

In this book, we have used the terms *'Memoization'* and *'Dynamic Programming'*, to refer to top-down and bottom-up approaches of problem solving where a subproblem is solved only once.

Iterative function to compute n^{th} Fibonacci term that we saw in Code 4.2 is actually a dynamic programming solution. We went in a bottom-up manner, starting with first computing `fib(1)`, then `fib(2)` and so on (moving in forward direction).

```
int fib(int n){
  if(n==1 || n==2)
     return 1;

  int a = 1; // For (k-2)'th term term.
  int b = 1; // For (k-1)'th term
  int c;     // For k'th term

  for (int i = 3; i <= n; i++)
  {
    c = a + b;
    a = b;
    b = c;
  }
  return c;
}
```

Code: 6.1

Both Memoization and Dynamic Programming solves indivisual subproblem only once.

Memoization uses recursion and work top-down, whereas Dynamic Programming moves in opposite direction solving the problem bottom-up.

Dynamic programming unroll the recursion and move in opposite direction to Memoization.

Code 6.1 takes linear time. Memoized function in Code 5.1 also takes $O(n)$ time, but DP is better because there is no recursive function call and only one instance of activation record gets created on the Stack.

Note that even Code 6.2 is DP.

```
int fib(int n){
  // Array to store fib numbers
  int arr[N];
```

```
arr[1] = 1;   arr[2] = 1;

for (int i = 3; i <= n; i++)
{
    // compute fib(n) and store it
    arr[i] = arr[i-1] + arr[i-2];
}

return arr[n];
}
```

Code: 6.2

But obviously it is less optimized than Code 6.1 because we are storing all the terms computed till now taking $O(n)$ extra memory. To compute the kth term, we only need $(k-1)^{th}$ term and $(k-2)^{th}$ term and not the previous terms. Code 6.2, unnecessarily increases extra memory consumption from $O(1)$ to $O(n)$.

Question 6.1. Write function to calculate `fibonacci(n)` in `lg(n)` time.

We have seen the recursive and memoiezed version of Example 4.2 in chapter 4 and Chapter 5. The recursive solution takes exponential time and memory and memoized version takes $O(n^3)$ time. However better solution is to use bottom-up DP approach that takes $O(n^2)$ time and $O(n)$ extra memory.

The approach is to first calculate min cost for Station-0, then for Station-1, then Station-2, and so on. These costs are stored in a one dimensional array `minCost[N]`.

Minimum cost to reach station-0 is zero, because we are already there
`minCost[0] = 0;`

Minimum cost to reach Station-1 is `cost[0][1]`, because that is the only way to reach Station-1
`minCost[1] = cost[0][1];`

Minimum cost to reach `Station-2` is minimum of below two values (either go directly to `Station-2` or take a break at `Station-1`).

```
1.    minCost[0] + cost[0][2]
2.    minCost[1] + cost[1][2]
```

Note that `MinCost` is a lookup in the cache and `cost` is a lookup in the `cost` array. Similarly, minimum cost to reach `Station-3` is minimum of below three values.

1. Go to `station-3` directly

```
      minCost[0]+cost[0][3]
```

2. Go to `station-1` then from there go to `station-3` directly

```
      minCost[1]+cost[1][3]
```

3. Go to `station-2` (min cost already computed) then go to `station-3`

```
      minCost[2]+cost[2][3]
```

When we are breaking at `station-2`. We are using the already computed min cost of reaching `station-2` and adding the actual cost of going directly from `station-2` to `station-3` (observe optimal substructure).

Similarly minimum cost to reach `Station-4` is minimum of 4 values

```
1.    minCost[0]+cost[0][4]
2.    minCost[1]+cost[1][4]
3.    minCost[2]+cost[2][4]
4.    minCost[3]+cost[3][4]
```

and so on. Code 6.3 has the function for this:

```
int calculateMinCost(int cost[N][N]){
  // minCost[i]=min cost from station-0 to station-i
  int minCost[N];
  minCost[0] = 0;
  minCost[1] = cost[0][1];

  for (int i=2; i<N; i++)
  {
    minCost[i] = cost[0][i];
```

```
    for(int j=1; j<i; j++)
      if(minCost[i] > minCost[j] + cost[i][j])
        minCost[i] = minCost[j] + cost[i][j];
  }
  return minCost[N-1];
}
```

Clearly, DP is the most optimal solution, in terms of both execution time and memory as seen in Fibonacci and min-distance problems.

Major applications of DP is in solving complex problems bottom-up where the problem has optimal substructure and subproblems overlaps. The challenge with Dynamic Programming is that it is not always intuitive esp. for complex problems. In Chapter-7 we discuss the strategy to nail down complex dynamic programming problems step-by-step.

Sometime the subproblems overlap in a non-obvious way and does not appear to have an intuitive recursive solution, as shown in the Example 6.1.

Example 6.1: Find length of longest substring of a given string of digits, such that sum of digits in the first half and second half of the substring is same. For example,
Input: "142124"
Output: 6

The whole string is answer, because, sum of first 3 digits = sum of last 3 digits $(1+4+2 = 1+2+4)$.
Input: "9430723"
Output: 4

Longest substring with first and second half having equal sum is "4307".

Solution

One hint is that result substring have even number of digits, since its first and second halves are equal in length.

The brute force solution is to consider all the substrings of even length and check if sum of digits in their first half is equal to that of second half.

In the process keep a check of the length of substrings and return maximum of all lengths at the end.

A small optimization can be that if we have already found a substring with length greater than current substring for which sum of two halves is equal, then we do not need to compute sum of left and right halves for current substring (see Code 6.4).

```c
int maxSubStringLength(char *str){
  int n = strlen(str);
  int maxLen =0;

  // i = Starting index of substring
  for(int i=0; i<n; i++)
  {
    // j = End index of substring (even length)
    for(int j =i+1; j<n; j += 2)
    {
      // len = Length of current Substring
      int len = j - i + 1;

      // If maxLen is > length of current string.
      // Do Nothing
      if(maxLen >= len)
        continue;

      int lSum = 0, rSum = 0;
      for(int k =0; k < len/2; k++)
      {
        lSum += (str[i+k] - '0');
        rSum += (str[i+k+len/2] - '0');
      }
      if(lSum == rSum)
        maxLen = len;
    }
  }
  return maxLen;
}
```

Code: 6.4

This function takes $O(n^3)$ time, and this is probably the first solution that strike our mind. Two important points from this example are:

1. The most intuitive solution may not always use recursion.
2. The most intuitive solution may not always take exponential time.

But there are subproblems and subproblems are overlapping.

For example, sum of digits from index i to j is already computed while checking for one substring. Then for another substring (in next loop) we may be computing sum of digits from index i+1 to j. We are computing this sum all over again when we can reusing the sum of digits from i to j and just subtract str[i] from this sum (constant time operation) rather then re-computing the sum from i+1 to j (linear time operation).

Let us build a two-dimensional table that stores sum of sub strings. sum[i][j] in Code 6.5 store sum of digits from index i to index j.

```
/* sum[i][j] = Sum of digits from i to j
 * if i>j, then value holds no meaning.
 */
int sum[N][N];

int maxSubStringLengthDP(char *str){
  int n = strlen(str);
  int maxLen = 0;

  // Lower diagonal of matrix is not used (i>j)
  // Filling diagonal values.
  for (int i =0; i<n; i++)
    sum[i][i] = str[i]-'0';

  for (int len=2; len<=n; len++)
  {
    // Pick i and j for current substring
    for (int i=0; i<n-len+1; i++)
    {
      int j = i+len-1;
      int k = len/2;
```

```
    // Calculate value of sum[i][j]
    sum[i][j] = sum[i][j-k] + sum[j-k+1][j];

    // Update if 'len' is even, left and right
    // sums are same and len is more than maxLen
    if (len%2 == 0 && sum[i][j-k] == sum[(j-k+1)][j]
                 && len > maxLen)
        maxLen = len;
    }
}
return maxLen;
}
```

Code: 6.5

The above solution is using DP and takes $O(n^2)$ time and $O(n^2)$ extra memory. Clearly there is a scope of improvement in terms of extra memory taken because we are not using lot of space that we have allocated in the 2-dim matrix.

Question 6.2: solve the problem in Example 6.1 so that it does not take more than $O(n^2)$ time and takes constant extra memory.

 INTERVIEW TIP

If someone does not know anything about Dynamic Programming then also he may be solving Example 5.2 the same way as we did. Just that we have a name for this type of approach. He may be just optimizing the memory and time taken by the brute-force solution.

As an analogy: Sometimes the approach we take for coding, the way we organize our classes and interfaces is such that it has its applicability at multiple places outside the current project also. So we document that way of coding and call it design pattern.

Someone completely unaware of a design pattern may also be solving the problem in a similar way. Just that he is not aware if it is called Design pattern or if it has any name.

In next chapter we look at the difference in two fundamental approaches of problem solving that we have discussed so far. The top-down approach (recursion or memoization) and bottom-up approach (dynamic programming).

7

Top-Down v/s Bottom-Up

Contrast is an excellent teacher.

We have learnt about recursion, memoization and dynamic programming in previous chapters. First two are top-down approach to problem solving while DP solves a problem in bottom-up manner. In this chapter we try to further compare bottom-up and top-down approaches of problem solving.

Example 7.1: Consider Code 7.1 to compute factorial of n.

```
int factorial(int n){
  if(1==n)
    return 1;
  else
    return n * factorial(n-1);
}
```

Code: 7.1

While defining the solution we have a top-down view. We define `factorial(n)` in terms of `factorial(n-1)` and then put a terminating condition at the bottom.

Picture 7.1 shows the function calls for `factorial(4)`. This is a top-down approach of problem solving. We start solving the problem from top (`factorial(4)`) and solve subproblems (at bottom) on need basis. If solution of a subproblem is not required for computing the solution of larger problem, then the subproblem is not solved.

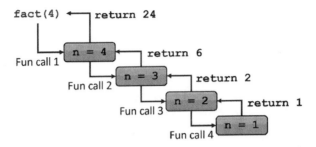

A bottom-up approach on the other hand develops the solution starting from the bottom as shown below:

```
1! = 1
2! = 2 (1!) = 1
3! = 3 (2!) = 6
4! = 4 (3!) = 24
```

```
int factorial(int n){
  int fact = 1;
  for(int i=2; i<=n; i++)
    fact *= i;
  return fact;
}
```

In top-down we have an understanding of the destination initially and we develop the means required to reach there. On the other hand, bottom-up has all the means available and we move toward the destination. Below is an interesting analogy:

Top-down: *First you say I will take over the world. How will you do that? You say, I will take over Asia first. How will you do that? I will take over India first. How will you do that? I will first become the Chief Minister of Delhi, etc. etc.*

Bottom-up: *You say, I will become the CM of Delhi. Then will take over India, then all other countries in Asia and finally I will take over the whole world.*

We saw the difference, right? No matter, how similar it looks, it has nothing to do with any Chief Minister ☺.

Note that in both approaches the first work done is Acquiring-Delhi. Similarly, factorial(1) will be computed first no-matter what the approach is. Just that in Top-down, we have a backlog of computing all the factorials (in memory Stack in form of activation records).

Top-down is usually more intuitive because we get a bird's eye view and a broader understanding of the solution.

The simplest example of top-down approach are Binary tree algorithms. The algorithm of pre-order traversal is:

PreOrder(Root)

    Print data at root

    Traverse left sub-tree in **PreOrder**

    Traverse right sub-tree in **PreOrder**

This algorithm, starts from the top and moves toward leaves. Most of the Binary tree algorithms are like this only. We start from the top, traverse the tree in some order and keep making decisions on the way. Consider the below example:

Example 7.2: Given a Binary Tree, For each node, add sum of all the nodes in its hierarchy to its value. Below picture shows a sample input and output.

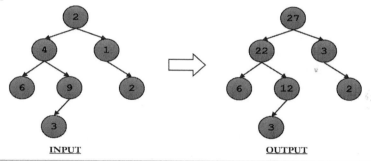

INPUT   OUTPUT

Picture: 7.2

Node with value 9 has only one child, its value get added to 9 and value of this node becomes 12. Node with value 4 has three nodes in its hierarchy (6, 9 and 3), all these values will get added to this node and final value of this node becomes = 4 + 6 + 9 + 3 = 22. Similarly, all other nodes, have their values updated. Leaf nodes remain unchanged.

Note: *this problem is not related to DP.*

In most Binary Tree questions, we do not have to solve the entire problem. If we look at it from top and assume that the problem is already solved for left and right sub trees, then we just need to solve it for the root node.

Recursion solves the problem for left and right subtrees and we just need to put the terminating condition(s). In this example there can be two terminating conditions:

1. If current node is null, do not do anything.
2. If current node is leaf node, then also do not do anything.

Algorithm is to traverse the tree in post order (because we will be adding the sum only after the problem is solved for both the child nodes) and solves the problem as discussed below.

addChildSum(Root)
>   **addChildSum** for Left sub-tree
>   **addChildSum** for Right sub-tree
>   **Add** value of left and Right child nodes to root

Code 7.3 translates above algorithm to code.

```
void addChildSum(Node * root){
    if(root == NULL) return; // Terminating cond.

    // Compute for Left Sub Tree
    addChildSum(root->left);

    // Compute for Right Sub Tree
    addChildSum(root->right);

    int finalSum = root->data;
    if(root->left != NULL)
        finalSum += root->left->data;

    if(root->right != NULL)
        finalSum += root->right->data;

    root->data = finalSum;
}
```

Code: 7.3

Nothing will change for leaf nodes. For all other nodes, after computation is done for left and right subtrees, we add the data of left and right child to the current node.

Note that, even if the algorithm is top-down, the flow of data is always bottom-up.

 *INTERVIEW TIP*

Recursion *is a top-down approach of problem solving.*

Memoization *is also top-down, but it is an improvement over recursion where we cache the results when a subproblem is solved, when same subproblem is encountered again we use the result from cache rather then computing it again. It has the drawbacks of recursion with an improvements that one problem is solved only once.*

So if there are no overlapping subproblems (eg. In the case of factorial function) memoized function will be exactly same as recursive function.

Dynamic programming *attempts to solve the problem in a bottom-up manner avoiding the overhead of recursion altogether.*

In almost all cases, bottom-up is better than top-down. But for the sake of completeness, let us discuss one use case where you may choose to go with top-down[16].

Negatives of Bottom-up DP

In top-down approach (recursion or memoized) we do not solve all the subproblems, we solve only those problems that need to be solved to get the solution of main problem. In bottom-up dynamic programming, all the subproblems are solved before getting to the main problem.

We may therefore (very rarely) be solving more subproblems in top-down DP than required. The DP solutions should be properly framed to remove this ill-effect. Consider the below example:

Example 7.3: In combinatorics, Combination is defined recursively:

```
C(n,m) = C(n-1,m) + C(n-1,m-1)
```

Code 7.4 defines recursive function that take two arguments n and m and return C(n,m).

---

[16] Such comparative knowledge is good to have from interview point of view. The interviewer have luxury of asking any question and expects a balanced answer from you. As a candidate you do not have that luxury.

```
int comb(int n, int m){

    if(n == 0 || m == 0 || (n == m))
        return 1;
    else
        return comb(n-1,m) + comb(n-1,m-1);

}
```

Code: 7.4

The DP solution for this problem requires to construct the entire pascal triangle and return the $(m+1)^{th}$ value in the $(n+1)^{th}$ row. (Row number and column number starts from zero). For example, $C(5,4)$ will return the highlighted value in below Pascal triangle:

```
              1
          1     1
        1    2    1
      1    3    3    1
    1    4    6    4    1
  1    5   10   10    5    1
```

The DP solution construct the whole triangle and return this value. The recursive solution on the other hand compute only the required nodes of Pascal triangle as highlighted below

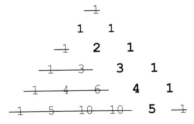

If n and m are very big values then recursion may actually beat DP, both in terms of time and memory.

This is just to complete the discussions, otherwise, if dynamic programming can be used, then go for it, it will almost never disappoint you.

We now know everything about Dynamic Programming. Next chapter focuses on the strategy used to solve dynamic programming problems asked in coding competitions or interviews.

8

Strategy for DP Question

Fitting-in is a short term strategy,
Standing out pays off in long term.

There is no magic formula, no shortcut !

The most important thing is methodical thinking and practice, *"practice good, practice hard"*.

Dynamic programming is an art and the more DP problems we solve, the easier it gets to relate a new problem to the one we have already solved and draw parallel between the two. It looks very artistic when we see someone solving a tricky DP so easily.

While solving a DP question, it is always good to write recursive solution first and then optimize it using either DP or Memoization depending on complexity of problem and time available to solve the problem.

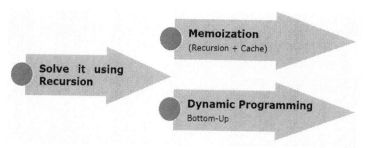

Dynamic programming problems has two properties, **optimal substructure** and **overlapping subproblems**. Optimal substructure property makes recursion an obvious choice to solve DP problems.

Most often, both Memoization and DP use the logic of Recursion only. These approaches are already discussed in previous chapters. In next sections we are just revising these three concepts with the help of an example.

Solve it Using Recursion

If we have a command over recursion, then we may be able to give a recursive solution to the DP problems without even knowing that they belong to DP. Consider the below example:

Example 8.1: Given a two-dimensional square matrix `cost[][]` of order M*N where `cost[i][j]` represents the cost of passing though cell(i,j). Total cost to reach a particular cell is the sum of costs of all the cells in that path (including the starting and final cell). We can only move either downward or rightward. i.e If we are at cell (i, j) then we can either go to cell (i, j+1) or to (i+1, j).

Write a function that return the minimum cost of moving from the top-left cell to bottom-right cell of the matrix. Picture 8.1 shows the Cost matrix and Minimum Cost path in that matrix.

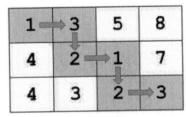

1	3	5	8
4	2	1	7
4	3	2	3

Cost Matrix   **MinCostPath**

Picture: 8.1

Without having any prior knowledge of Dynamic Programming, we can solve it by applying methodical problem solving approach.

In recursion, we start solving from the last cell, define the larger problem in terms of the smaller subproblems of the same type and call the same function recursively to solve the subproblems.

- **Larger Problem:** get the minimum path cost till cell (2,3)
- **Smaller Problems-1:** get the minimum path cost till cell (2,2)
- **Smaller Problems-2:** get the minimum path cost till cell (1,3)

The smaller-problems are exactly same as larger problem with different values of M and N. The same function that solve large problem can also solve smaller problems. Hence, Recursion !

Once we have solution to smaller problems, we know the minimum cost to reach cell $(2,2)$ and minimum cost to reach cell $(1,3)$. Now, There are only two ways to reach the last cell $(2,3)$ and they are via cell $(2,2)$ and cell $(1,3)$

If x and y are the minimum cost to reach cell $(2,2)$ and $(1,3)$ respectively, then minimum cost of reaching cell $(2,3)$ is

MINIMUM(x, Y) + Cost[2][3]

Let us write the above logic in the form of code

```
int minPathCost(int cost[M][N], int m, int n){
    int x = minPathCost(cost, m-1, n);
    int y = minPathCost(cost, m, n-1);
    return (getMin(x,y) + cost[m][n]);
}
```

Code: 8.1

getMin is a helper function that returns minimum of two integers. We need to add terminating condition in the above code. Below are the terminating conditions ((m,n) represent the destination cell):

1. If m=0 and n=0, it means our destination is top-left cell only. there is only one way to be at $(0,0)$ cell. Return value stored at cell $(0,0)$.

2. If m=0 and n≠0, we are in the top row and not at $(0,0)$. The only way to reach this cell is from right because there is no way to reach it from the top. Calculate the minPathCost of cell on the right and add current cell's cost.

3. If m≠0 and n=0, we are in the first column (leftmost) and not at $(0,0)$. Then the only way to reach this cell is from top because there is no way to reach it from the right. Calculate the minPathCost of cell above it and add current cell's cost.

Point 2 and 3 above are not exactly terminating conditions. They are just restricting the recursion. Point 1 is the only terminating condition. Code 8.2 is the complete code with all terminating conditions.

```
int getMin(int a, int b){
  return a<b?a:b;
}
// calculate the min path cost from (0,0) to (m,n)
int minPathCost(int cost[M][N], int m, int n){

  if(m == 0 && n == 0)   // At cell (0,0)
    return cost[0][0];

  if(m == 0) // IN FIRST ROW
    return minPathCost(cost,m,n-1) + cost[0][n];


  if(n == 0) // IN FIRST COLUMN
    return minPathCost(cost,m-1,n) + cost[m][0];


  int x = minPathCost(cost, m-1, n);
  int y = minPathCost(cost, m, n-1);
  return (getMin(x,y) + cost[m][n]);
}
```

Code: 8.2

In the interviews, even this solution may be acceptable to the interviewer, esp. if the candidate is less experienced.

Also, observe the optimal substructure property in Code 8.2. The optimal solution of larger problem depends on the optimal solutions of smaller subproblems.

Problem with Code 8.2 is that solutions of subproblems are computed multiple times. For example, minPathCost for index $(1, 2)$ is computed twice in the given example. Picture 8.2 shows the function call diagram for M=2, N=3.

Numbers in each node represent the value of M, N for which the function is called. The diagram is not complete for the sake of saving space, but in the diagram itself, we are computing the minPathCost of reaching cell $(1, 2)$ twice. All the function calls under the subtree with cell $(1, 2)$ are duplicate.

If values of M and N are large, there will be lot of overlaps and as expected, Code 8.2 takes exponential time, $O(2^n)$. And since it involves recursion, the extra memory taken is also very high.

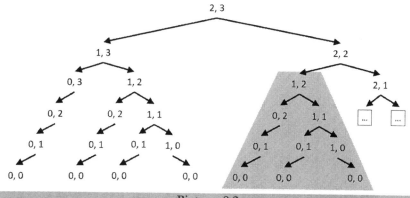

Picture: 8.2

Memoized Approach (Recursion + Remember)

A better approach is to remember the solution of `minPathCost` for each cell (i, j) when it is computed for the first time in some cache (2-dim array). When we want `minPathCost` for cell (i,j) again, then we just look-up into the cache rather than computing it all over again. Since we are storing cost for each cell, storing it in a two-dim matrix makes the most obvious choice. Code 8.3 is the memoized version of Code 8.2:

```
// Global cache used to store memoized results.
int MEM[M][N] = {0};

int minPathCost(int cost[M][N], int m, int n){
  // If the value for cell (m,n) is already
  // computed, don't compute it again.
  if(MEM[m][n] != 0){
    return MEM[m][n];
  }

  if(m == 0 && n == 0){
    MEM[m][n] = cost[0][0];
  }
  else if(m == 0){
    MEM[m][n] = minPathCost(cost, m, n-1)+cost[0][n];
  }
  else if(n == 0){
    MEM[m][n] = minPathCost(cost, m-1, n)+cost[m][0];
```

```
}
else{
    int x = minPathCost(cost, m-1, n);
    int y = minPathCost(cost, m, n-1);
    MEM[m][n] = (getMin(x,y) + cost[m][n]);
}
    return MEM[m][n];
}
```

Code: 8.3

Note: *In the above code we have used a global array MEM to store results of subproblems. The problem with using global array is that we need to set all it's cells to zeros each time before calling function* minPathCost *otherwise it will hold values from the previous function call. We have kept it global for the sake of simplicity.*

Let us look at some important points:

1. When minPathCost is computed for any cell (i,j) for the first time, we store this value in MEM array at MEM[i][j].

2. Before computing the minPathCost for any cell (i,j), we check if that value is already computed or not (i.e MEM[i][j] is non-zero). If already computed, we just return that value and do not compute it again.

In Code 8.3 we are still using recursion, but not computing one problem multiple times. Picture 8.3 shows function call diagram for Code 8.3. Compare it with Picture 8.2, the number of function calls have reduced substantially.

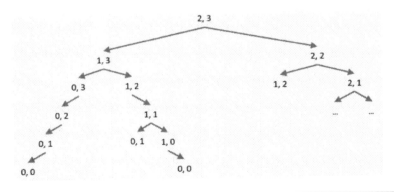

Picture: 8.3

Compare it with Picture 8.2. Total number of function calls have reduced substantially. Time taken by Code 8.3 is $O(n^2)$. If we consider a larger matrix (of say, $100*100$), then the difference between recursion and memoization is huge. In the next section we look into DP solution of this problem.

Bottom-Up DP Solution

The optimal solution is to move bottom-up[17] starting from $(0,0)$ to (m,n) and keep finding minPathCost for all the cells that fall in our way.

As in case of recursion, to compute the minPathCost of a particular cell, we need minPathCost of the cell above it and cell on left of it. We will fill the matrix as follows.

1. minPathCost of $(0,0)$ is same as cost[0][0]

1			

2. There is only one way to reach elements in the first row (from left). Hence the cost is sum of all the cells on the left added to value of the cell.

1	4	9	17

3. Similarly, there is only one way to reach cells in the first column, and that is from the top. Hence the minPathCost of all cells in the first column is sum of all the cells above it added to cell's value.

1	4	9	17
5			
9			

---

[17] Do not get confused by the name 'Bottom-Up'. It means that we are moving from the base case (or source) to the advanced case (or destination).

4. Now we need to fill rest of the empty cells starting from cell $(1, 1)$. The logic used is same as the one we used in recursion and memoization.

```
MEM[i][j] = getMin(MEM[i-1][j], MEM[i][j-1]) +
                cost[i][j];
```

Code 8.4 has the complete code of Dynamic Programming.

```
int MEM[M][N] = {0};
int minPathCost(int cost[M][N]){
  MEM[0][0] = cost[0][0];

  // Top Row
  for(int j=1; j<N ; j++)
    MEM[0][j] = MEM[0][j-1] + cost[0][j];

  // Left Column
  for(int i=1; i<M ; i++)
    MEM[i][0] = MEM[i-1][0] + cost[i][0];

  // Filling other cells
  for(int i=1; i<M; i++)
    for(int j=1; j<N; j++)
      MEM[i][j] = getMin(MEM[i-1][j], MEM[i][j-1]) +
                    cost[i][j];
  return MEM[M-1][N-1];
}
```

Code: 8.4

Code 8.4 does not use recursion and takes $O(n^2)$ time. It is a huge improvement over previous two versions, recursion and memoization.

Each cell of final `minPathCost` matrix (MEM) stores the minimum cost to reach that cell from $(0, 0)$

1	4	9	17
5	6	7	14
9	9	9	12

Picture: 8.4

Question 8.1: What will be the logic if we are allowed to move in three directions, right, down and diagonally lower cells.

Problem Solving Using DP

In some cases, we are expected to solve the problem using DP only. Rest of this chapter discuss how to identify if a problem is actually DP, and approaches that can be used to solve DP problems. Chapter-9 has practice questions that shows the strategy in action.

Before devising a strategy, first thing is to identify if a question is fit for DP.

Finding if DP is Applicable?

The strongest check for DP is to look for optimal substructure and overlapping subproblems.

DP is used where a complex problem can be divided in subproblems of the same type and these subproblems overlap in some way (either fully or partially). The overlap may be obvious as seen in Example 8.1 or non-obvious as in Example 6.1.

Most of the times, we may also be trying to optimize something, maximize something, minimize something or finding the total number of ways of doing something and the optimal solution for larger parameter depends on optimal solutions of same problems with smaller parameter.

Largest application of Dynamic programming is in solving complex problems that demonstrate **Overlapping subproblems** and **Optimal substructure**.

Ask yourself the following questions:

1. Is it possible to divide the problem into subproblems of the same type?

2. Are the subproblems overlapping?

3. Are we trying to optimize something, maximizing or minimizing something or counting the total number of possible ways to do something.

If the answer to first two questions is yes, chances are that DP is applicable. Take the third point as a bonus check.

Solving DP Problems

There is no one fool-proof plan that we can use to solve all DP questions because not every problem is the same, but one should be able to solve most DP problems following the below steps:

1. **See if DP is applicable.** If problem can be defined in terms of smaller subproblems and the subproblems overlap then chances are that DP can be used.

2. **Define recursion.** Having subproblems of similar kind means there is recursion.

    a) **Define problem in terms of subproblems**, define it in a top-down manner, do not worry about time complexity at this point.

    b) **Solve base case (leave rest to recursion).** The subproblems are solved by recursion, what is left is the base case.

    c) **Add a terminating condition.** This step is relatively trivial. We need to stop somewhere. That will be the terminating conditions.

    After this step we have a working solution using recursion.

3. **Try memoization (optional).** If a subproblem is solved multiple times, then try to cache its solution and use the cached value when same subproblem is encountered again.

4. **Try solving Bottom-up.** This is the step where we try to eliminate recursion and redefine our solution in forward direction starting from the most basic case. In the process we store only those results that will be required later.

Step-3 is usually for the beginners, who are just starting with the concept. It is an improvement over step-2 without getting into the complexity of DP. In interviews, usually the recursive solution is acceptable, but the best answer is DP. In the coding competitions, usually DP is the only accepted solution. With experience we start skipping step-3 and jump to step-4 directly.

 INTERVIEW TIP

At point-2 we have a working solution. It may be taking more time than the optimal solution, but it is syntactically and semantically correct.

It may be sufficient to solve the problem till this point during an interview. But you should apprise the interviewer that it is not the most optimal solution and you can further optimize it by using DP.

Let us see this strategy in action in some real interview questions:

Example 8.2: Given an empty plot of size 2 x n. We want to place tiles such that the entire plot is covered. Each tile is of size 2 x 1 and can be placed either horizontally or vertically. If n is 5, then one way to cover the plot is as shown in Picture 8.6

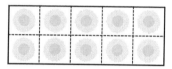 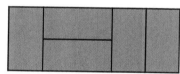

Empty plot   **Tiles placed in Plot**

Picture: 8.6

Write a function that accept n as input and return the total number of ways in which we can place the tiles (without breaking any tile).

Solution

Let us define the recursion. We can place the tile either horizontally or vertically.

1. If we place the first tile vertically, then the problem reduces to:
   Number of ways tiles can be placed on a plot of size 2*(n-1).

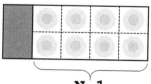

N-1

Picture: 8.7

2. If we place the first tile horizontally, then the second tile must also be placed horizontally (see Picture 8.9). The problem then reduces to: *Number of ways tiles can be placed on a plot of size 2*(n-2).*

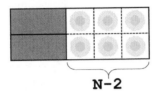

N-2

Picture: 8.8

In both the cases we are able to define the large problem in terms of smaller problems of the same type. This is Recursion. Recursion also has terminating conditions. Terminating conditions are:

```
If n==1, there is just 1 way possible
```
✓ Place one tile vertically
```
If n==2, there are 2 possible ways
```
✓ Place both tiles vertically
✓ Place both tiles horizontally.

Code 8.5 has the recursive solution for this problem:

```
int countWays(int n){
    // terminating conditions
    if(n == 0) { return 0; }
    if(n == 1) { return 1; }
    if(n == 2) { return 2; }
    return countWays(n-1) + countWays(n-2);
}
```

Code: 8.5

The above recursion is same as that of Fibonacci (except for the terminating conditions). The dynamic solution to Fibonacci was discussed in Code 6.1 and is an O(n) time solution.

 INTERVIEW TIP

It is a good idea during the interview if you can relate the unknown problem to a known problem. You can even tell this to the interviewer. This is a big quality and will go in your favor while deciding for your selection.

Question 8.2: If size of the plot in Example 8.2 is changed to 3*n, then what changes do we need to make in the solution? Picture 8.9 shows one of the possible arrangements on a plot of size 3*n where n=12.

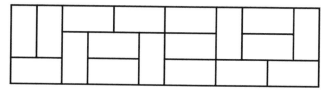

Picture: 8.9

Example 8.3: Consider a game where a player can score 3, 5 or 10 points in one move. Given a total score N, find the total number of unique ways to reach a score of N.

For example: If N = 13, output should be 5 because there are 5 ways to reach to a score of 13 as shown below

```
(3, 10)    (3, 5, 5)    (5, 3, 5)    (5, 5, 3)    (10, 3)
```

The recursion to solve this problem is

```
#of ways to score N = #of ways to score (N-10) +
                      #of ways to score (N-5)  +
                      #of ways to score (N-3)
```

With the below terminating conditions:
1. #of ways to score N is 0 if n<0
2. #of ways to score N is 1 if n == 0

The code is simple

```
int waysToScore(int n){
  if(n < 0) { return 0; }
  if(n == 0) { return 1; }

  return waysToScore(n-10) +
         waysToScore(n-5) +
         waysToScore(n-3);
}
```

Code: 8.6

Code 8.6 is solving one subproblem multiple times. The function call tree for n=13, is shown in Picture 8.10. The tree is not complete, but it shows that subproblems overlap, and as n becomes large, there will be more overlaps. Code 8.6 takes exponential time, $O(n^3)$ in the worst case.

Code 8.7 gives bottom-up dynamic programming solution for this problem. It uses one-dimensional array, arr and store number of ways to score k at index k in the array.

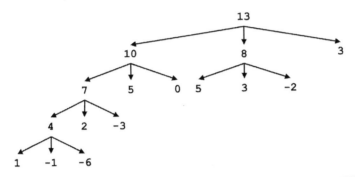

Picture: 8.10

```
int waysToScore(int n){
    // arr[i] will store numberOfWays to score i.
    int arr[n+1] = {0}, i;

    arr[0] = 1;

    for(i=1; i<=n; i++)
    {
        if(i-3 >= 0)
            arr[i] += arr[i-3];
        if(i-5 >= 0)
            arr[i] += arr[i-5];
        if(i-10 >= 0)
            arr[i] += arr[i-10];
    }

    return arr[n];
}
```

Code: 8.7

Question 8.3: What is the total number of ways to reach a particular score if (10, 3) and (3, 10) are considered same. Modify your function accordingly.

Consider one more example

Example 8.4: Given an array of integers, write a function that returns the maximum sum of sub array, such that elements are contiguous.
Input Array: {-2, -3, 4, -1, -2, 1, 5, -3}
Output: 7

        (-2, -3, **4, -1, -2, 1, 5**, -3)

The brute-force algorithm for this problem is given in Code 8.8. It use two loops and consider all intervals (i,j) of the array for all possible values of i and j.

```
int maxSubArraySum(int * arr, int n){
  int maxSum = 0;
  int tempSum = 0;

  for(int i=0; i<n; i++)
  {
    tempSum = arr[i];
    for(int j=i+1; j<n; j++)
    {
      // tempSum hold sum of all elements from
      // i to j index (both including)
      tempSum += arr[j];
      if(tempSum > maxSum)
        maxSum = tempSum;
    }
  }
  return maxSum;
}
```

Code: 8.8

If all the elements of array are negative, then above algorithm returns 0. This may not be acceptable, we can add one more check at the end to see if maxSum is 0. In this case, we set maxSum to maximum value in the array.

Kadane's Algorithm

Code 8.8 takes $O(n^2)$ time. There is a better algorithm to solve this problem. It is called Kadane's Algorithm. It is $O(n)$ time algorithm and requires the array to be scanned only once. We keep two integer variables

```
int maxSumEndingHere = 0;
int maxSumSoFar = 0;
```

Loop for each element in the array and update the two variables as shown below:

```
maxSumEndingHere = maxSumEndingHere + a[i]
if(maxSumEndingHere < 0)
    maxSumEndingHere = 0
if(maxSumSoFar < maxSumEndingHere)
    maxSumSoFar = maxSumEndingHere
```

Code 8.9 is the complete code:

```
int maxSubArraySum(int a[], int n){
  int maxSumSoFar = 0;
  int maxSumEndingHere = 0;

  for (int i = 0; i < n; i++)
  {
    maxSumEndingHere  = maxSumEndingHere  + a[i];

    if (maxSumEndingHere  < 0)
      maxSumEndingHere  = 0;

    if (maxSumSoFar < maxSumEndingHere)
      maxSumSoFar = maxSumEndingHere;
  }
  return maxSumSoFar;
}
```

Code: 8.9

The function takes $O(n)$ time and is an improvement over the previous one. If we call this function for the following array

```
{-2, -3, 4, -1, -2, 1, 5, -3}
```

Then the intermediate values of `maxSumEndingHere` and `maxSumSoFar` variables are shown in Table 8.1 below:

Table: 8.1

This is one of the few examples of dynamic programming where brute force solution is non-recursive and is relatively easy. In fact the recursion of this problem is unintuitive. The recursion is defined below

i	maxSumEndingHere	maxSumSoFar
0	0	0
1	0	0
2	4	4
3	3	4
4	1	4
5	2	4
6	7	7
7	4	7

```
M(n) = max(M(n-1) + A[n], A[n])
```

Where `M` is the function, `maxSubArraySum` and `A` is the array. The optimal substructure property of problem is clear from above equation, to find the `maxSubArraySum` for n elements we need to find `maxSubArraySum` of n-1 elements. But subproblems are not overlapping because `M(n)` is only calling `M(n-1)`.

This leaves room for interpretations as to whether Kadane's algorithm is DP or not. It demonstrates the optimal substructure property by breaking larger problem down into smaller subproblems, but its core recursive approach does not generate overlapping subproblems, which is what DP is meant to handle efficiently.

We do not have a strong opinion on this, readers are free to opine whether or not they consider Kadane's algorithm as DP. If such discussion comes in the interview, then take it as an opportunity to give both sides of the story along with your stand point. Such technical discussions are as important as answering any question in the interview.

9

Practice Questions

Edit Distance

Example 9.1: The words COMPUTER and COMMUTER are very similar, and a **update** of just one letter, P->M will change the first word into the second. Similarly, word SPORT can be changed into SORT by **deleting** one character, p, or equivalently, SORT can be changed into SPORT by **inserting** p.

Edit distance between two strings is defined as the minimum number of character operations (update, delete, insert) required to convert one string into another.

Given two strings str1 and str2 and following three operations that can performed on str1.

1. Insert
2. Remove
3. Replace

Find minimum number of operations required to convert str1 to str2. For Example: if Input strings are CAT and CAR then the edit distance is 1

REPLACE

Similarly, if the two input strings are, SUNDAY and SATURDAY, then edit distance is 3.

INSERT INSERT   REPLACE

Recursive Solution

As discussed earlier in the book, we try to define the larger problem in term of smaller problems of the same type. We start with comparing the first character of str1 with first character of str2.

- If they are same, then we do not need to do anything for this position and need to find the edit distance between remaining strings (ignoring first character from each).

- If they are not same, then we can perform three operations:

  - **Delete** first character of str1 and find edit distance between str2 and str1 (with first character of str1 removed).

  - **Replace** the first character of str1 with first character of str2 and then find the edit distance between the strings ignoring first character from each string (because they are same).

  - **Insert** the first character of string str2 at the head of string str1. After insertion, the first character of of two strings become same and we need to find edit distance between the two strings ignoring their first characters. (size of str1 has increased by one character)

We find the minimum of these values using recursion. Since we have already applied one operation (either of Delete, Replace or Insert), add one to this minimum value and return the result.

Code 9.1 is the code for above recursion:

```
int editDistance(char* str1, char* str2){
  // If str1 is empty,
  // then all characters of str2 need to inserted.
  if(str1 == NULL || *str1 == '\0')
    return strlen(str2);

  // If str2 is empty,
  // then all characters of str1 need to be deleted.
  if(str2 == NULL || *str2 == '\0')
    return strlen(str1);

  // If first characters of both are same,
  // then ignore it and find edit distance
  // of rest of the strings
  if(*str1 == *str2)
    return editDistance(str1+1, str2+1);

  // Find edit distance for all three operations
  int d, u, i;
  d = editDistance(str1+1, str2);
  u = editDistance(str1+1, str2+1);
  i = editDistance(str1, str2+1);

  // Return minimum of the three values plus 1
  return getMinimum(d, u, i) + 1;
}
```

Code: 9.1

Code 9.1 takes exponential time in the worst case, $O(n^3)$ to be precise and there are lot of overlapping subproblems as shown in Picture 9.1. The diagram show function calls for two string of size 3 each that gives the worst case time. For example, str1 = "ABC", str2 = "XYZ" editDistance of last 2 characters from each string (2,2) is computed three time. If the string sizes are big then there will be further overlap of subproblems.

Dynamic Solution

The dynamic solution to the above problem solves for all possible combinations of two strings in bottom-up. If `str1` has n characters and `str2` has m characters then total number of possible combinations are m*n. This makes matrix of order m*n an obvious choice to store the `minEditDistance` of subproblems.

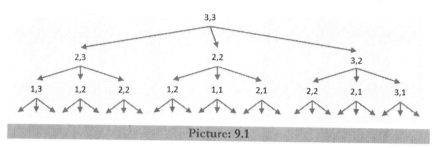

Picture: 9.1

In such cases, where we have two strings and we want to store some value corresponding to each cell (i,j) that have i characters from first string and j characters from second string, we put one string in the row and other in the column.

Picture 9.2 show it for strings "SUNDAY" and "SATURDAY"

		S	A	T	U	R	D	A	Y
S									
U				C_{ij}					
N									
D									
A									
Y									

Picture: 9.2

Each cell represents the minimum edit operations needed for the corresponding first and second strings. For example, Cell marked as C_{ij} in Picture 9.2, store number of edit operations required if two strings are "SAT" and "SU" respectively. When all cells of the matrix are populated, then bottom-right cell will hold the minimum edit distance between two strings SATURDAY and SUNDAY.

First empty row represents the edit distances when first string is empty, and the second empty column represents edit distances when second string is empty[18].

The top row and leftmost column are easy to fill. If the first string is empty, then all the characters of second string need to inserted in first or all characters from second need to be deleted to make the two same. In both the cases, number of operations is equal to the number of characters in second string. Similarly first column is filled with number of characters in the first string.

		S	A	T	U	R	D	A	Y
	0	1	2	3	4	5	6	7	8
S	1								
U	2								
N	3								
D	4								
A	5								
Y	6								

Picture: 9.3

Let us call above matrix EditD. Then remaining cells of this matrix are populated as below:

```
IF (str1[i-1] == str2[j-1])
  EditD[i][j] = EditD[i-1][j-1]
ELSE
  EditD[i][j] = 1 + MINIMUM(EditD[i-1][j-1],
                            EditD[i-1][j],
                            EditD[i][j-1])
```

Code 9.2 below is the code for above logic:

```
int editDistDP(char* s1, char* s2, int m, int n){
  int EditD[m+1][n+1];

  for(int j=0; j<=m; j++)     // TOP ROW
    EditD[0][j] = j;

  for(int i=0; i<=n; i++)     // LEFT COLUMN
```

---

[18] You may skip the empty top row and empty leftmost column and change your logic accordingly.

```
      EditD[i][0] = i;

  for (int i=1; i<=m; i++){
    for (int j=1; j<=n; j++){
      // IF TWO CHAR ARE SAME
      if (s1[i-1] == s2[j-1])
        EditD[i][j] = EditD[i-1][j-1];
      else
        EditD[i][j] = getMinimum(EditD[i][j-1],
                       EditD[i-1][j],
                       EditD[i-1][j-1]) + 1;
    }
  }
  return EditD[m][n];
}
```

Code: 9.2

If we follow above logic, matrix is populated as shown in Picture 9.4:

		S	A	T	U	R	D	A	Y
	0	1	2	3	4	5	6	7	8
S	1	0	1	2	3	4	5	6	7
U	2	1	1	2	2	3	4	5	6
N	3	2	2	2	3	3	4	5	6
D	4	3	3	3	3	4	3	4	5
A	5	4	3	4	4	4	4	3	4
Y	6	5	4	4	5	5	5	4	3

Picture: 9.4

Code 9.2 takes $O(n^2)$ time and $O(n^2)$ extra memory. It is a huge improvement over the $O(3^n)$ exponential time solution of Code 9.1. Just to get a sense of difference, if $n=100$, then $3^n = 5.1537752e+47$ and n^2 is just 10000.

Total Path Count

Example 9.2: Given a two dimensional array, find total number of paths possible from top-left cell to bottom-right cell if we are allowed to move only rightward and downward. For example, if matrix is of order 2*2, then only two paths are possible as shown in Picure 9.5.

In a matrix of order 3*4, there are 10 unique paths to reach cell (2,3) from (0,0), two of these paths are shown in Picture 9.6.

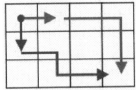

| Picture: 9.5 | Picture: 9.6 |

Solution

This problem is very similar to the one discussed in Example 8.1. The approach to solve this problem is also similar.

Recursive Solution

The cell (m,n) can be reached from two cells

1. The one above it (m-1, n)
2. The one on the left of it (m, n-1)

Suppose if there are P1 ways of reaching cell (m-1, n) and P2 ways of reaching cell (m,n-1), then we can reach cell (m,n) in P1 + P2 unique ways, via cell (m,n-1) and (m-1,n). This defines our recursion.

The terminating condition is when we hit the top row or leftmost column. There is just one way to reach any cell in top row (going rightward from (0,0)). Similarly, there is only one way to reach any cell in the leftmost column (going downwards from (0,0)). The number of ways to reach (0,0) is zero because we are already there.

These can be the terminating conditions of our recursion. Code 9.3 implements this recursive logic.

```
int numOfPaths(int m, int n){
    // TERMINATING CONDITIONS
    if(m == 0 && n == 0){return 0;} // CELL (0,0)
    if(m == 0 || n == 0){return 1;} // FIRST ROW/COLUMN
```

```
return  numOfPaths(m-1, n) + numOfPaths(m, n-1);
}
```

Code: 9.3

Code 9.3 takes exponential time, $O(n^2)$. Clearly, it demonstrates both the properties of DP, optimal substructure and overlapping subproblems. The dynamic solution of this problem is also similar to the DP solution of Example 8.1.

Dynamic Solution

We take two-dimensional array as cache and first populate top row and left column as per terminating conditions.

0	1	1	1
1			
1			

Now, we start populating rest of the cells as
`arr[i][j] = arr[i-1][j] + arr[i][j-1]`

The final matrix is

0	1	1	1
1	2	3	4
1	3	6	10

Each cell `(i,j)` represent the total nummber of paths to reach that cell from top-left cell `(0,0)`. The last cell `(2,3)` holds the final value.

```
int numOfPathsDP(int m, int n){
    // Variable length arrays allowed in C language. If
    // your compiler gives error, allocate it on heap.
    int cache[m][n];

    for (int i = 1; i < m; i++) // 1st Row
        cache[i][0] = 1;
```

```
for (int j = 1; j < n; j++) // 1st Column
    cache[0][j] = 1;

// populating other cells
for (int i = 1; i < m; i++)
    for (int j = 1; j < n; j++)
        cache[i][j] = cache[i-1][j] + cache[i][j-1];

return cache[m-1][n-1];
}
```

Code: 9.4

Code 9.4 takes $O(n^2)$ time. Using DP we have reduced the time taken from exponential to polynomial.

Question 9.1: Given a 2-dim grid where there is a horizontal and a vertical road after each kilometer as shown in Picture 9.7. Dotted lines show the roads.

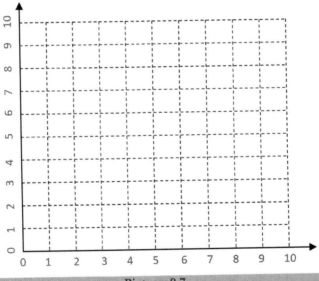

Picture: 9.7

You are at the origin $(0,0)$, and want to go to a point (x,y). What is the total number of unique routes that you can take if you are allowed to move only in forward and upward directions?

Question 9.2: A variation to the problem asked in Question 9.1 is that, at some places there is repair work going on and hence you cannot take those routes. Unavailable route information may be given in the form of point array (e.g from point $(2,1)$ to point $(3,1)$ the route is not available).

In the below diagram, cross represent blocked route. If cross is placed on a particular edge then that edge is not allowed.

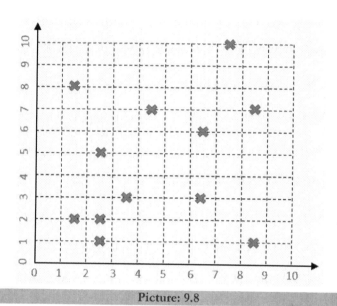

Picture: 9.8

Write a function that returns the total number of unique ways to go to some point (x,y) from origin $(0,0)$.

Question 9.3: What if in Example 9.2, you are allowed to move in diagonal direction also? How will your logic change for recursive and dynamic solution? Same variation can be asked for Question 9.1 and Question 9.2.

Question 9.4: Minimum Chess Moves Problem. In the game of chess a Knight can move 2.5 steps (a square that can be reached by moving two squares horizontally and one square vertically, or two squares vertically and one square horizontally). Picture 9.9 shows all possible moves of a knight. A King, can move only one step (either horizontally, vertically or diagonally). Valid moves of a king is shown in Picture 9.10.

We have designed a special piece that can move either like a knight or like a king. If that piece is named P, then all valid moves of P are shown in

Picture 9.11. It is union of moves of Knight and King.

Given that P is in a particular cell, and you want to move it to another cell then what is the minimum number of moves it takes P to go from source to destination. Write a function that accepts source and destination cells and return the minimum number of moves it will take P to move from source to destination cell.

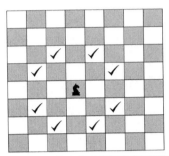
Picture: 9.9

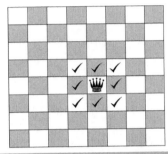
Picture: 9.10

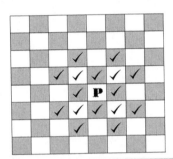
Picture: 9.11

String Interleaving

Example 9.3: String C is said to be interleaving of string A and B if it contains all the characters of A and B and the relative order of characters of both the strings is preserved in C. For example, if values of A, B and C are as given below.

```
A = xyz    B = abcd
C = xabyczd
```

string C is the interleaving of strings A and B as shown in Picture 9.12:

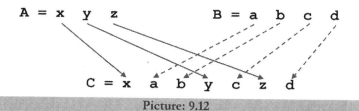

Picture: 9.12

Given three string A, B and C, write a function to check if third string is the interleaving of first and second strings.

Solution

One of first checks should be that,

> IF (num of char in C $\neq$ num of char in A + num of char in B) THEN C IS NOT interleaving of A and B.

When the number of characters in C is equal to sum of number of characters in other two strings only then we need to move forward.

The approach to solve this problem is simple, consider the three strings again and check each character of string C
```
A = xyz    B = abcd
C = xabyczd
```

The first character x, in C obviously comes from string A, because the first character of B is not x. The problem now reduce to, check if string abyczd is an interleaving of string yz and abcd. i.e
```
A = yz  B = abcd
C = abyczd
```

This problem is of same type as original problem and can be solved using recursion. Another case is when first character of both A and B is same as that of C, consider below values for A, B and C:
```
A = bcc    B = bbca
C = bbcbcac
```

In this case, first character of C can either come from A or from B and we have to look for both the possibilities as shown in Picture 9.13.

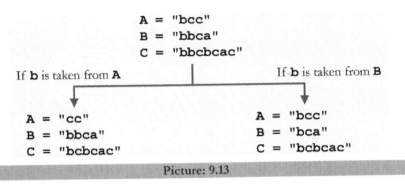

A = "bcc"
B = "bbca"
C = "bbcbcac"

If **b** is taken from **A**   If **b** is taken from **B**

A = "cc"   A = "bcc"
B = "bbca"   B = "bca"
C = "bcbcac"   C = "bcbcac"

Picture: 9.13

In both the cases the problem is getting reduced to the subproblems of the same type, hence **optimal substructure**. The subproblems are also overlapping as shown in Picture 9.14.

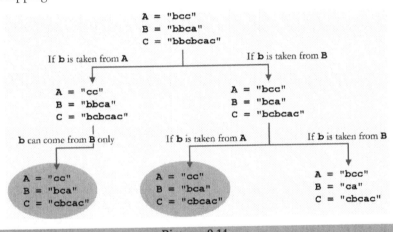

A = "bcc"
B = "bbca"
C = "bbcbcac"

If **b** is taken from **A**   If **b** is taken from **B**

A = "cc"   A = "bcc"
B = "bbca"   B = "bca"
C = "bcbcac"   C = "bcbcac"

b can come from **B** only   If **b** is taken from **A**   If **b** is taken from **B**

A = "cc"   A = "cc"   A = "bcc"
B = "bca"   B = "bca"   B = "ca"
C = "cbcac"   C = "cbcac"   C = "cbcac"

Picture: 9.14

The subproblems marked with circle are exactly same. This subproblem is solved twice while computing solution of the main problem. If strings are large then there will be many such **overlapping subproblems**.

Hence it is a fit case for Dynamic Programming. Let us write the recursive solution first:

Below is the recursive function that accepts three string A, B and C and return true if string C is interleaving of strings A and B.

```
int isInterleaving(char* A, char* B, char* C)
{
  // If all strings are empty
  if (!(*A) && !(*B) && !(*C))
```

```
      return true;

   // If C is empty, A or B (or Both) is not empty
   if (*C == '\0')
      return false;

   // If both A and B are empty, but C is not
   if(*A == '\0' && *B == '\0')
      return false;

   int first = false;
   int second = false;

   // If first char of A = first char of C
   if(*A == *C)
      first = isInterleaving(A+1, B, C+1);

   // If first char of B = first char of C
   if(*B == *C)
      second = isInterleaving(A, B+1, C+1);

   return (first || second);
}
```

Code: 9.5

True and false are defined as 1 and 0 respectively.Code 9.5 takes $O(2^n)$ exponential time. Below, we discuss the DP solution to reduce this time to polynomial time.

Dynamic Programming Solution

The dynamic solution starts solving the problem bottom-up. At each stage we are computing if a substring of C is interleaving of substrings of A and B. If i (i<=m, length of A) and j (j<=n, length of B) are variables that iterate over string A and B then for all possible values of i and j we see if first i characters of A and first j characters of B interleave to form first (i+j) characters of C.

91

Matrix seems to be the obvious choice for storing all such values (Because there are two parameters i and j) with one string on horizontal axis and one on vertical axis as shown in Picture 9.15.

	b	b	c	a
b				
c				
c				

Picture: 9.15

The value in the cell (i, j) is true if first i characters of A and first j characters of string B interleave to form first (i+j) characters of string C. While filling the matrix, if we are at cell (i, j), we check the (i+j-1)th character in C.

For example, cell (1, 2) represent whether b (first 1 char of bcc) and bb (first 2 characters of string bbca) interleave to form bbc (first 3 characters of string bbcbcac) or not. In our solution this should be false because they do not interleave to form bbc.

Cell (0, 0) is true. It means that zero characters of A and zero characters of B interleave to form string that is same as first zero characters of string C.

	b	b	c	a
	T			
b				
c				
c				

Picture: 9.16

First row means that string A is empty. It will just check if substring B is same as that of substring of C:

```
IF (B[i-1]!= C[i-1])
    MAT[0][i] = FALSE
```

```
ELSE
    MAT[0][i] = MAT[0][i-1]
```

Similarly First column will be populated as

```
IF (A[j-1]!= C[j-1])
    MAT[j][0] = FALSE
ELSE
    MAT[j][0] = MAT[j-1][0]
```

The first row and column for strings bcc, bbca and bbcbcac are populated as shown in Picture 9.17.

		b	b	c	a
	T	T	T	T	F
b	T				
c	F				
c	F				

Picture: 9.17

Other cells are populated starting from top-left, moving in row-wise order. At each cell, we compare the current character of A and B with the current character of C. if we are at cell (i, j), then current characters of A, B and C are the $i-1^{th}$, $j-1^{th}$ and $(i+j-1)^{th}$ character in A, B and C respectively. At each cell, there are four possibilities

1. Current character of C is neither equal to current character of A nor current character of B. Value of cell is False.

2. Current character of C is equal to current character of A, but not current character of B. Value of cell is same as the cell above it.

3. Current character of C is equal to current character of B, but not current character of A. Value of cell is same as the cell on its left.

4. Current character of C is equal to current character of both A and B (all three are same). Value of cell is true if either the cell above it or on the left of it is true, otherwise it is false.

Code 9.6 has the complete code.

```
bool isInterleaved(char* A, char* B, char* C)
{
```

```
// Find lengths of the two strings
int M = strlen(A);
int N = strlen(B);

// c should have exactly M+N characters
if(strlen(C) != M+N)
   return false;

// 2-Dim Array Mat.
// All values are set to 0 (FALSE)
bool Mat[M+1][N+1];

Mat[0][0] = true;

// Populating first column
for(int i=1; i<=M; i++)
{
  if(A[i-1] != C[i-1])
    Mat[i][0] = false;
  else
    Mat[i][0] = Mat[i-1][0];
}

// Populating first Row
for(int j=1; j<=N; j++)
{
  if(B[j-1] != C[j-1])
    Mat[0][j] = false;
  else
    Mat[0][j] = Mat[0][j-1];
}

for (int i=1; i<=M; ++i)
{
  for (int j=1; j<=N; ++j)
  {
    // Cur char of C same as A but not B
```

```
if(A[i-1]==C[i+j-1] && B[j-1]!=C[i+j-1])
{
  Mat[i][j] = Mat[i-1][j];
}
// Cur char of C same as B but not A
else if(A[i-1]!=C[i+j-1] &&
        B[j-1]==C[i+j-1])
{
  Mat[i][j] = Mat[i][j-1];
}
// Cur char of C same as both A and B
else if(A[i-1]==C[i+j-1] &&
        B[j-1]==C[i+j-1])
{
  Mat[i][j]=(Mat[i-1][j] || Mat[i][j-1]) ;
}
else
{
  Mat[i][j] = 0; // FALSE
}
}
}

  return Mat[M][N];
}
```

Code: 9.6

After all the cells are populated the matrix will look like Picture 9.18. Final answer is the value stored in bottom-right cell.

		b	b	c	a
	T	T	T	T	F
b	T	T	F	T	F
c	F	T	T	T	T
c	F	F	T	F	T

C = b b c b c a c

Picture: 9.18

Code 9.6 takes $O(n^2)$ time. This is a huge improvement over the exponential time recursive solution.

Question 9.5: Given two strings, print all the interleavings of the string. For example,

```
INPUT: AB XY
OUTPUT: ABXY AXBY AXYB XABY XAYB XYAB
```

Question 9.6: In Example 9.3, if all the characters in string A are different from those in string B, then do we still need the two-dimensional matrix? Suggest a $O(n+m)$ time algorithm that takes $O(1)$ extra memory and gives the right result for this particular case.

Subset Sum

Example 9.4: Given an array of non-negative integers and a positive number X, determine if there exist a subset of the elements of array with sum equal to X. For example:

```
Input Array: {3, 2, 7, 1}    X = 6
Output: True // because sum of (3, 2, 1) is 6
```

Solution:

The recursive solution is relatively easy, if we traverse the array, then, at each element, there are two possibilities, either to include that element in the sum or not. If current element in the array is P, then

- If we include it in the sum, we need to search for X-P in remaining array.

- If we do not include it in the sum, we need to search for X in the remaining array.

In both the cases, we are left with a similar type of problem that can be solved using recursion. The terminating condition for recursion is when either X becomes 0 (success) or array is exhausted (failure). Consider code 9.7.

```
int isSubsetSum(int* arr, int n, int X)
{
  if (X == 0)
    return true;
```

```
if (n == 0)
   return false;

// If first element is > X, ignore it
if (arr[0] > X)
   return isSubsetSum(arr+1, n-1, X);

/* else, check both ways
 *  - excluding first element in the sum
 *  - including first element in the sum
 */
return  isSubsetSum(arr+1, n-1, X) ||
        isSubsetSum(arr+1, n-1, X-arr[0]);
}
```

Code: 9.7

Clearly the subproblems are overlapping and recursion is taking exponential time $O(2^n)$. DP can help improve upon this time.

Dynamic Programming Solution

In DP we solve it in a bottom-up manner and store intermediate results in a two dim matrix MAT[][]. MAT[i][j] is true if there is a subset of arr[0 .. i] with sum equal to j, otherwise false. The final value will be in MAT[n][X].

If array is {3, 2, 7, 1} and X is 6, then we have one column of matrix for sum going from 0 to X and a row for each element of the array as shown in picture 9.19

	0	1	2	3	4	5	6
3							
2							
7							
1							

Picture: 9.19

First column is all true, because if X is 0 then we can always make up that with an empty set (not picking any element from array). The first row is all false except for the place where X=3, because with one 3, we can only

97

form a sum of 3 and nothing else (for 6 we need two 3's, but we just have one in this subarray).

	0	1	2	3	4	5	6
3	T	F	F	T	F	F	F
2	T						
7	T						
1	T						

Picture: 9.20

We fill all other cell in row-wise order (starting with cell $(1,1)$). While populating the ith row, if v is the value of ith row (ex. v for row-0 is 3, for row-1 is 2, for row-2 is 7 and row-3 is 1) then first v positions in the row are exact copy of the row above it because value of the row cannot contribute in those values.

	0	1	2	3	4	5	6
3	T	F	F	T	F	F	F
2	T	F					
7	T						
1	T						

Picture: 9.21

For all other columns, we again look in the row above it:

- IF value at cell just above it, i.e $(i-1, j)$, is True then cell (i,j) is also True.
- ELSE, copy the content of cell $(i-1, j-v)$ to cell (i,j).

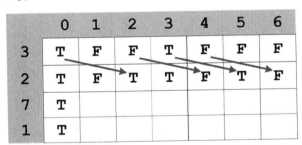

	0	1	2	3	4	5	6
3	T	F	F	T	F	F	F
2	T	F	T	T	F	T	F
7	T						
1	T						

Picture: 9.22

Note that the cell $(1,3)$ is true because the cell just above it is true. After filling all values in the matrix, it will look like below

	0	1	2	3	4	5	6
3	T	F	F	T	F	F	F
2	T	F	T	T	F	T	F
7	T	F	T	T	F	T	F
1	T	T	T	T	T	T	T

This row is exact copy of the previous row because
7 does not contribute in sum when X is 6.

Picture: 9.23

The final answer is the value in the bottom-right cell of the matrix.

```
int isSubarrSum(int arr[], int n, int X)
{
  // The value of MAT[i][j] is true if there is a
  // MAT of arr[0..j-1] with X equal to i
  int MAT[X+1][n+1];

  // If X is 0, then answer is true
  for (int i = 0; i <= n; i++)
    MAT[0][i] = true;

  // If X is not 0 and arr is empty, answer is false
  for (int i = 1; i <= X; i++)
    MAT[i][0] = false;

  // Fill the MAT table in botton up manner
  for (int i = 1; i <= X; i++)
  {
    for (int j = 1; j <= n; j++)
    {
      MAT[i][j] = MAT[i][j-1];
      if (i >= arr[j-1])
        MAT[i][j] = MAT[i][j] ||
                    MAT[i - arr[j-1]][j-1];
    }
  }
  return MAT[X][n];
}
```

Code: 9.8

Question 9.7: Given an array of numbers and a number X, find two numbers whose sum is equal to X. Your solution should take not more than $O(n.lg(n))$ time and constant extra memory in the worst case. Do you need DP in this case?

Question 9.8: In Example 9.4, we are just returning a boolean value true or false. We are not actually printing the subset that sum up to X. For example, if array is {3, 2, 7, 1} and X is 6, the function returns true, but it will not print the subset (3, 2, 1) whose sum is 6.

Write a function the prints the subset and return true if there exist a subset whose sum is equal to X. If no such subset exists, then the function should not print anything and just return false.

Longest Common Subsequence

Example 9.5: A subsequence of a string S, is a set of characters that appear in the string in left-to-right order, but not necessarily consecutively. For example if string is ACTTGCG

- Then, ACT , ATTC , T , ACTTCG are all subsequences,

- But, TTA is not Subsequence of the string.

A string of length n can have 2^n subsequences (including the null sequence and the entire array[19]).

A **common subsequence** of two strings is a subsequence that is subsequence of both strings. A longest common subsequence (LCS) is a common subsequence of maximal length. For example if S1 and S2 are two sequences as given below:

S1 = AAACCGTGAGTTATTCGTTCTAGAA

S2 = CACCCCTAAGGTACCTTTGGTTC

---

[19] If string is "ABC", then at each character we have two choices, either to include that character in the subsequence or not. And these two choices will result in two different subsequences. Hence the total number of subsequences are,

$2 * 2 * 2 = 8$.

It is similar to finding the power set of a set.

Then their LCS is `ACCTAGTACTTTG` that is present in both the sequences:

```
S1 = AAACCGTGAGTTATTCGTTCTAGAA
S2 = CACCCCTAAGGTACCTTTGGTTC
```

Given two strings, write a function that returns the total number of characters in their Longest Common Subsequence (LCS). In above example, the function should return 13, number of characters in LCS `ACCTAGTACTTTG`. If the given strings are `ABCD` and `AEBD` then this function should return 3, length of the LCS, `ABD`.

Recursive Solution

The problem demonstrate optimal substructure property and the larger problem can be defined in terms of smaller subproblems of the same type (and hence recursion).

Let m and n be the total number of characters in the two strings respectively. We start with comparing the last characters of these two strings. There are two possibilities:

1. **Both are same**
    Then this character is the last character of their LCS. It means we have already found one character in LCS. Add 1 to the result and remove the last character from both the strings and make recursive call with the modified strings.

2. **Both are different**
    Then we need to find lengths of two LCS, first having of m-1 characters from first string and n characters from second string and another with m characters from first string n-1 characters from the second string, and return the maximum of two.

Case 1:

```
LCS("ABCD", "AEBD") = 1 + LCS("ABC", "AEB")
```

Case 2:

```
LCS("ABCDE", "AEBDF") = Max(LCS("ABCDE", "AEBD"),
                            LCS("ABCD", "AEBDF"))
```

Consider one more example, when S1 is ABCDEF and S2 is APQBRF their last characters are same, so

LCS (ABCDEF, APQBRF) = 1 + LCS(ABCDE, APQBR)

Now the two sequences that we have are ABCDE and APQBR. Their last characters are not same, hence,

LCS(ABCDE, APQBR) = MAX (LCS(ABCDE, APQB),
                          LCS(ABCD, APQBR))

And so on. Let us code this logic in C language

```c
int lcs(char *X, char *Y, int m, int n)
{
  // terminating condition of recursion
  if (m == 0 || n == 0)
    return 0;

  // Comparing last character of strings
  if (X[m-1] == Y[n-1])
    return 1 + lcs(X, Y, m-1, n-1);
  else
    return getMax (lcs(X, Y, m, n-1),
                   lcs(X, Y, m-1, n));
}
```

Code: 9.9

Where getMax is a function that returns maximum of two integer values as defined below:

```c
int getMax(int x, int y){
    return (x > y)? x : y;
}
```

Code 9.9 takes exponential time, $O(2^n)$ in the worst case and worst case happens when all the characters of the two strings are different (in case of mismatch function is called twice).

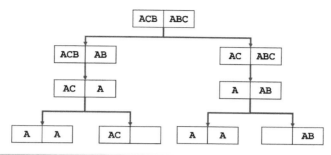

Picture: 9.24

Picture 9.24 shows that we are solving one subproblem multiple times. So, the LCS problem demonstrates optimal substructure, and there are overlapping subproblems also. It is a fit case for DP. We first talk about how to memoize it and then look at the DP solution.

Memoization

To avoid computation of a subproblem multiple times we can either use memoization or dynamic programming. In memoization, we take a two dimensional array, of size M*N

```
int table[m][n];
```

When length of LCS of first i characters of X and j characters of Y is computed for the first time, it is stored in cell table[i][j]. If function is called with m=i and n=j again then the LCS is not computed from scratch and stored value is returned from the table. Below code uses memoization, for the sake of simplicity, table is defined global[20]. Let us assume that all cells in the table are initialized with -1.

Note that, since table is global, we have to initialize it each time, before calling the function, else it will use the values populated in last function call.

```
int lcs(char *X, char *Y, int m, int n)
{
    // terminating condition of recursion
```

----

[20] As discussed earlier also, usually it is not a good practice to declare global variable and it is certainly bad to have it global in this case. The calling function need to re-initialize table with -1 each time before the call, else, it will continue to hold values from previous function call.

```
if (m == 0 || n == 0)
   return 0;

// If value is already computed
if(table[m][n] != -1)
   return table[m][n];

// Comparing last character of strings
if (X[m-1] == Y[n-1])
   table[m][n] = 1 + lcs(X, Y, m-1, n-1);
else
   table[m][n] = getMax (lcs(X, Y, m, n-1),
                 lcs(X, Y, m-1, n));
   return table[m][n];
}
```

Code: 9.10

We have reduced the time complexity from exponential to polynomial time, but the function in Code 9.10 is still using recursion. Next we discuss the DP solution that solve the problem bottom-up without using recursion.

Using bottom-up DP, the problem can be solved in $O(mn)$ time, i.e $O(n^2)$ if both strings has n characters.

Dynamic Programming Solution

The bottom-up solution builds the table of LCS of substrings and start computing the length building on the final solution. As in other such cases, we use a matrix and place one string along the row and another one along the column as shown in the below diagram for strings ABCD and AEBD.

	Φ	A	E	B	D
Φ	0	0	0	0	0
A	0				
B	0				
C	0				
D	0				

First row represents the case when first string is empty, and first column represents the case when second string is empty.

In both cases the LCS will have zero characters because one of the two strings is empty.

Let, name of the table above be `LCSCount`, we start populating it in row-wise order using the following logic:

```
IF (str1[i-1] == str2[j-1])
    LCSCount[i][j] = LCSCount[i-1][j-1] + 1;
ELSE
    LCSCount[i][j] = max(LCSCount[i-1][j],
                         LCSCount[i][j-1]);
```

After the matrix is populated it will look like Picture 9.25 and final value is in the bottom-right cell of the `LCSCount` matrix.

	φ	A	E	B	D
φ	0	0	0	0	0
A	0	1	1	1	1
B	0	1	1	2	2
C	0	1	1	2	2
D	0	1	1	2	3

Picture: 9.25

Code 9.11 shows the above DP logic in action. We may not receive m and n as parameters because there are library functions to compute length of a string.

```
int LCS(char *str1, char *str2, int m, int n){
    // All cells of matrix are initialized to 0.
    // So, don't need explicit initialization
    // for first row and column.
    int LCSCount[m+1][n+1];

    // making first col zero
    for(int i=0; i<=m; i++)
        LCSCount[i][0] = 0;

    // making first row zero
    for(int j=0; j<=n; j++)
        LCSCount[0][j] = 0;

    for (int i=1; i<=m; i++)
```

105

```
{
    for (int j=1; j<=n; j++)
    {
      if (str1[i-1] == str2[j-1])
        LCSCount[i][j] = LCSCount[i-1][j-1] + 1;
      else
        LCSCount[i][j] = max(LCSCount[i-1][j],
                             LCSCount[i][j-1]);
    }
}
    return LCSCount[m][n];
}
```

Code: 9.11

The above code takes O(mn) time to execute and is an improvement over both recursion and memoization.

Example 9.6: Extend the solution of Example 9.5 to also print the LCS. For example, in the above example, the function should also print ABD.

Solution:

While filling the LCSCount matrix, we remember from where the value of each cell is coming. For any cell in the matrix, value may be:

1. Same as the cell on left side of current cell.

2. Same as the cell above the current cell.

3. 1 + value of cell on left-up of current cell.

For each cell, if we look at where the value in that cell is being populated from (above, left or diagonally upward). The value is populated from diagonally upward when current characters of both strings are same, as shown in Picture 9.26. Else it is populated from the larger of the two values, one above it and second on the left of it.

After matrix is populated (using Code 9.11), we start from bottom-right cell and move upward tracing the path till top row (or left column) as shown in Picture 9.27.

	φ	A	E	B	D
φ	0	0	0	0	0
A	0	1	1	1	1
B	0	1	1	2	2
C	0	1	1	2	2
D	0	1	1	2	3

Picture: 9.26

	φ	A	E	B	D
φ	0	0	0	0	0
A	0	1	1	1	1
B	0	1	1	2	2
C	0	1	1	2	2
D	0	1	1	2	3

Picture: 9.27

While moving backward, whenever we move diagonally upward, we add that character to the start of LCS. The LCS in above case is ABD.

Let us assume that LCSCount is defined globally. LCS function, when called will populate this matrix. The code for printing the longest common subsequence is shown in Code 9.12. It calls the function LCS from Code 9.11.

```
int printLCS(char *str1, char *str2, int m, int n)
{
  // Will populate the LCSCount array.
  int len = LCS(str1, str2, m, n);

  // Array to store the char in LCS
  char lcs[len+1];
  lcs[len] = '\0'; // last char
  len--;

  // Start from bottom-right corner
  int i = m, j = n;
  // Continue till we hit the top or left wall
  while (i > 0 && j > 0)
  {
    // If current char in str1 and str2 are equal,
    // then, it is part of LCS
    if (str1[i] == str2[j])
    {
      lcs[len] = str1[i];
      i--; j--; len--;
    }
```

107

```
// If not equal, find larger of the two and
// go in direction of larger value
else if (LCSCount[i-1][j] > LCSCount[i][j-1])
  i--;
else
  j--;
}


// Print the lcs
printf("LCS is :%s", lcs);
}
```

Code: 9.12

If we ignore the time taken by the LCS function, the core logic of Code 9.12 takes $O(n)$ time. Because at each point we are moving one step. And we need to move only n steps in worst case (the LCS cannot have more characters than the length of original sequence).

Question 9.9: Given an array of integers write code that returns length of the longest monotonically increasing subsequence in the array.

Question 9.10: Change Question 9.9 to also print longest monotonically increasing subsequence in the array.

Question 9.11: A sequence is bitonic if it is first monotonically increases and then monotonically decreases. For example, the sequences $(1,4,6,8,3,-2)$, $(9,2,-4,-10,-15)$, and $(1,2,3,4)$ are all bitonic, but $(1,3,12,4,2,10)$ is not bitonic.

Write a function that accepts an array of integers and returns the length of longest bitonic subsequence in the array.

Please note that a sequence in increasing order is bitonic with empty decreasing part and similarly a sequence in decreasing order is bitonic with empty increasing part.

Hint: A bitonic sequence can be circularly shifted to monotonically increase (or monotonically decrease sequence).

Question 9.12: Change Question 9.11 to also print the longest bitonic subsequence in an array.

108

Coin Change Problem

Example 9.7: Given an infinite supply of coins of N diffetent denominations (values), (V1, V2, ..., VN). Find the minimum number of coins that sum upto a number S. For example:

```
Input: Coins = {1, 2, 5, 10, 20, 50}, S = 65
Output: 3 (50+10+5)

Input: Coins = {1, 2, 5, 10, 12, 20, 50}, S = 65
Output: 3 (50+10+5)

Input: Coins = {1, 5, 6, 9}, S = 11
Output: 2 (6+5)
```

Greedy Approach

First of all the Greedy algorithm of taking the coin with highest demonination and subtracting its multiple from the total does not work in all cases. It will work fine for the coins of denominations that we have in our currency (even after demonetization).

Our currency has following denominations: 1, 2, 5, 10, 20, 50, 100, 500, 2000[21].

If we want to give a change of, say, 65 using minimum number of currency notes, then we can use the below greedy approach:

"Choose the maximum denomination possible"

We can check that this greedy approach give us the most optimal solution for given currency notes.

50, 10, 5

---

[21] When first draft of this book was written, in sept 2016, India had currency note of Rs. 1000 also. But after demonetization, these are the currency notes available in India.

Proof of correctness of above algorithm

Let C50, C20, C10, C5, C2 and C1 respectively, be the number of fifties, twenties, tens, fives, twos and ones in the change generated by the greedy algorithm and let Co50, Co20, Co10, Co5, Co2 and Co1, respectively, be the number of fifties, twenties, tens, fives, twos and ones in the change generated by an optimal algorithm.

We make the following observations:

The number of lower denomination is less that the value of next higher denomination. i.e the change given in Rs. 1 notes will be less than Rs. 2, because if it is equal to two then we will give a Rs. 2 note. Similarly number of Rs.2 notes will be less than 3 (because three Rs. 2 notes will make the value of six and hence Rs. 5 note will be used instead). Therefore,

C20 < 3, C10 < 2, C5 < 2, C2 < 3 and C1 < 2

In the optimal change solution, we can establish, similar thing. i.e

Co20 < 3, Co10 < 2, Co5 < 2, Co2 < 3 and Co1 < 2

To see this, note that is Co20 >=3, we can replace three twenties by a fifty and a ten and provide the change using one less currency note. Similarly,
we can say for the other denominations. Hence, the total amount of change given in lower denominations is less than the value of the next higher denomination.

Now if C50 != Co50, then either the greedy or the optimal solution must provide Rs. 50 or more in lower denominations. This violates the above observations. So, C50 = Co50. Similarly, if C20 != Co20, then either the greedy or the optimal solution must provide Rs. 20 or more in lower denominations which violates the above observations, so, C20 = Co20. Similarly we can prove it for other denominations.

Greedy do not work in all situations

In the greedy approach, we are not examining all possible solutions, the way we do in dynamic programming. Hence, only some specific problems can be solved using greedy approach. For other problems we may have to get back to dynamic programming.

For example, if we change the denomination of coins in the above problem to the following

```
{1, 2, 5, 10, 12, 20, 50}
```

And apply the same greedy approach

"Choose the maximum denomination possible"

Then we will give the following changes for S=65

First, we will give a note of Rs. 50. The value left is Rs. 15 and hence we cannot give any note of Rs. 20. So we will give a note of Rs. 12. Hence the currency given till now is: 50, 12

Rs. 3 more need to be given. There is no currency of Rs. 3. Hence we will give a change of 2 and 1. So we end up giving 4 currency notes as below:

```
50, 12, 2, 1
```

We know that the most optimal solution for S=65 has 3 currency notes:

```
50, 10, 5
```

Hence, the Greedy approach does not work for all the cases.

Recursive Solution

The minimum number of coins for a value of S can be computed using below recursive formula.

```
IF S == 0, THEN
    0 coins.
ELSE
    minCoins(S) = 1 + min(minCoins(S - coin[0]),
                          minCoins(S - coin[1]),
                          minCoins(S - coin[2]),
                          ... ...
                          minCoins(S - coin[N-1])
                         )
```

Coin array stores values of each currency denomination. In the above recursion, we are finding all possible solutions and then returning the minimum of all these values.

We are solving subproblems multiple times in the above recursion. For example, if inputs are

```
Coins = {1, 5, 6, 9},    S = 11
```

We can reach to a value of 6 by subtracting one 5 times or by subtracting 5 once from S. The subproblem for S=6, is solved multiple times.

Code 9.13 is the recursive code

```
int minCoins(int *coin, int n, int S){
  // Terminating Condition
  if (S == 0)
    return 0;

  // Initialize result
  int res = INT_MAX;
  for (int i=0; i<n; i++)
  {
    // Try every coin that has value < S
    if (coin[i] <= S)
    {
      int temp = minCoins(coin, n, S-coin[i]);

      if (temp + 1 < res)
        res = temp + 1;
    }
  }
  return res;
}
```

Code: 9.13

This solution is taking exponential time in the worst case. If we draw the function call tree, we can observe that subproblems are solved multiple times. That makes it a good candidate for Dynamic Programming.

We can also use memoization to avoid solving one subproblem again.

Just take an array of size S and when `minCoins` is computed for any value k for the first time, it is stored at index k in the array. When the function is called again for S = k, then a lookup happens in the array and this value is not computed again. Next is the Dynamic Programming solution:

Dynamic Programming Solution

In the DP solution, logic remain similar to recursion, just that the solution is computed in forward order, starting from i=1 to i=S.

```
int minCoins(int* coin, int n, int S)
{
  // resultArr[i] store minimum number of coins
  // required for S=i.
  // resultArr[S] will have final result.
  int resultArr[S+1];

  // For S=0
  resultArr[0] = 0;

  // Initialize all values to Infinite
  for (int i=1; i<=S; i++)
    resultArr[i] = INT_MAX;

  // Compute values bottom-up
  for (int i=1; i<=S; i++)
  {
    // Go through all coins < i
    for (int j=0; j<n; j++)
      if (coin[j] <= i)
      {
        int temp = resultArr[i-coin[j]];
        if(temp!=INT_MAX && temp+1 < resultArr[i])
          resultArr[i] = temp + 1;
      }
  }
  return resultArr[S];
}
```

Code: 9.14

Question 9.13: Update Example 9.7 to find total number of ways we can make the change of the amount using the coins of given denominations.

Cutting a Rod

Example 9.8: Given an iron rod of a certain length and price of selling rods of different lengths in the market, how should we cut the rod so that the profit is maximized.

For example, let us say that the price of rods of different lengths in the market is as given in the table below:

Length	1	2	3	4	5	6	7	8
Price	1	5	8	9	10	17	17	20

If we have a rod of length 4, then selling the rod as it is (without cutting it into pieces) in the market will get us value 9. Where as if we cut the road in two pieces of length=2 each, then the two pieces will be sold for Rs. 5 each, giving us a total value of 10 (5+5). Hence, it is a good idea to cut the rod in two pieces rather then sell it as a single piece in the market.

But we are still not sure if cutting rod in two equal pieces is the most optimal solution or not, because we have not seen all possible values. Since we are cutting the rod in integer lengths only, Table 9.1 lists all possible ways of cutting the rod and the cost of that combination in the market.

Length of each part	Total market value
4	9
1, 3	1+8=9
1, 1, 2	1+1+5=7
1, 1, 1, 1	1+1+1+1=4
2, 2	5+5=10

Table: 9.1

From Table 9.1, it is clear that cutting the rod in two equal pieces of length 2 each gives us the maximum value.

 INTERVIEW TIP

An important question that you should be asking to the interviewer is that whether or not there is any cost associated with cutting the rod. We have assumed it to be free, but during

the interview try to either ask explicitly, or if you assume it, then apprise the interviewer about your assumptions.

Another question that can be asked is if you can cut the rod in fractions or only integer length pieces are allowed.

Solution

The recursive solution is based on computing all possible combinations and value associated with each combination, and returning the maximum of all these values.

We cut the rod in all possible sizes and compare the cost as done in the code below:

```
// value array holds the market value of each length
// n is total length of the Rod.
// (We need values till length n)
int cutRod(int *value, int n)
{
  if (n <= 0)
    return 0;

  int maxValue = INT_MIN;

  for (int i=1; i<=n; i++){
    maxValue = getMaximum (maxValue,
                    value[i] + cutRod(value, n-i));
  }

  return maxValue;
}
```

Code: 9.15

Code 9.15 gives the right solution, but we are computing maxValue of one size again and again. Picture 9.28 shows the function calls for n=4. The maxValue of length 2 is computed twice. If n is large then there will be many overlapping subproblems. The solution takes exponential time because of these overlapping subproblems.

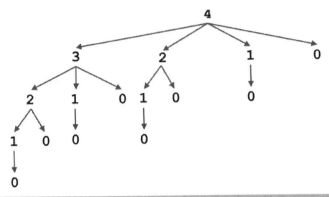

Memoized Solution

In memoization, we store the result of subproblem when it is computed for the first time and then reuse this result when the same subproblem is encountered again.

To store the results of subproblems use another array `maxValues` of size n. For the sake of simplicity, let us assume that this array is defined in global scope. The ith index of this array holds the `maxValue` for a rod of length i. Before computing the `maxValue` for length i, it will be checked in the table, whether value for i is already computed or not. If already computed, `resultArr[i]` is returned and not computed again as shown in Code 9.16.

```
// Array holds maxValue of length i at index i.
int maxValues[N] = {0};

int cutRod(int *value, int n){
  if (n <= 0)
    return 0;

  // If maxValue already computed
  if(maxValues[n] != 0)
    return maxValues[n];

  maxValues[n] = INT_MIN;
```

```
    for (int i=1; i<=n; i++){
      maxValues[n] = getMax(maxValues[n],
                          value[i] + cutRod(value, n-i));
    }


    return maxValues[n];
}
```

Code: 9.16

The above code will return the result in polynomial time, but it is still not the most optimized code because it is using recursion. Next is the optimized DP that solves the problem interatively.

Dynamic Programming Solution

In the dynamic programming we solve the problem starting from length 0, moving forward till length N.

```
int cutRod(int *values, int n){
  // Array holding the Max Values of i
  int maxValues[n+1];
  maxValues[0] = 0;

  int i, j;

  // Calcualting values from 1 to n
  for (i = 1; i<=n; i++)
  {
    int maxValues[i] = INT_MIN;
    for (j = 0; j < i; j++){
      maxValues[i] = max(maxValues[i],
                    values[j] + maxValues[i-j-1]);
    }
  }

  return maxValues[n];
}
```

Code: 9.17

If N=8 and value of each length is as given below:

Length	1	2	3	4	5	6	7	8
Price	1	5	8	9	10	17	17	20

Then the maxValue of each length as stored in maxValues array are as follows:

Length	0	1	2	3	4	5	6	7	8
maxValues	0	1	5	8	10	13	17	18	22

Dynamic programming solution takes $O(n^2)$ time and is an improvement over exponential time recursive solution.

0-1 Knapsack Problem

Example 9.9: Given n items in a shop, where each item has a weight and a value. A thief breaks into the shop with a knapsack. The thief can carry a maximum weight C. Items cannot be broken or taken partially. Each item has to be either picked or left completely. What is the maximum value that the thief can carry?

Let the below two arrays represent weight and value of each item

```
int W[n]; // WEIGHT ARRAY
int V[n]; // VALUE ARRAY
```

W[i] represent weight of ith item and V[i] represent the value of ith item. We have to find out the maximum value that the thief can carry.

Solution

Brute force solution is to consider all subsets of items and calculate total weight and value for each subset. Discard the subsets whose total weight is greater than C. From the remaining, pick the maximum value subset.

Recursive Solution

There are two options at the level of each item, this item is included in the final set (that thief carries) and this item is not included in the final set. We are computing two values:

1. When that item is included in the final set

2. When that item is not included in the final set

If the nth item is included in the final set, it means that thief has added that item to his knapsack. Then we need to find the maximum value thief can carry if there are $n-1$ items and he can carry a total weight of C-W[n-1]. Where W[n-1] is the weight of nth item

If the nth item is not included in the final set, it means that the thief has decided not to pick that item. Then we need to find the maximum value thief can carry if there are $n-1$ items and he can carry a total weight of C.

These two approaches leave us with subproblems of the same type. Below is the code for above recursion:

```
int knapSack(int C, int *weight, int *val, int n){
   // Terminating condition for recursion
   // If either no item left or knapsack is full
   if (n <= 0 || C <= 0)
      return 0;

   // If weight of the n'th item is more than C,
   // then it cannot be included in the knapsack.
   if (weight[n-1] > C)
      return knapSack(C, weight, val, n-1);

   // n'th item included
   int x = val[n-1] +
           knapSack(C-weight[n-1],weight,val,n-1);

   // n'th item not included
   int y = knapSack(C, weight, val, n-1);

   return getMax(x, y);
}
```

Code: 9.18

Code 9.18 takes exponential time, $O(2^n)$ in the worst case and the recursion will draw a very familiar function call tree where each node has two child nodes resulting in solving one subproblem multiple times.

DP Solution

One of the challenges of DP is to identify how to store the values. Usually, while storing the values, we keep on dimension for each solution variable.

Here we have two variable C(capacity) and N(items). Let row denote items and column denote the capacity. Cell (i,j) stores max value that thief can carry if first i items are in the shop and capacity of knapsack is j.

Code 9.19 below has the logic of populating the table.

```
int knapSack(int C, int *weight, int *val, int n){
  int table[n+1][C+1];

  // top row and first col will hold zero
  for(int i=0; i<=n; i++)
    table[i][0] = 0;
  for(int j=1; j<=C; j++)
    table[0][j] = 0;
  for (int i = 1; i <= n; i++)
  {
      for (int cp = 1; cp <= C; cp++)
      {
      if (weight[i-1] <= cp)
      {
        int x = cp-weight[i-1];
        table[i][cp]=getMax(val[i-1] + table[i-1][x],
                       table[i-1][cp]);
      }
      else
        table[i][cp] = table[i-1][cp];
      }
  }
  return table[n][C];
}
```

Code: 9.19

Code 9.19 takes `O(nC)` time. If we have four items (`n=4`) with the following weight and values

weight	2	3	4	5
Value	3	4	5	6

And capacity is 5 (`C=5`). Then the table is populated as below:

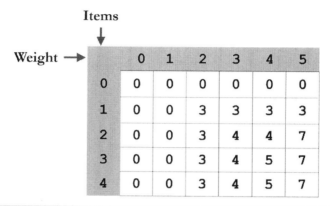

Items

Weight →

Weight	0	1	2	3	4	5
0	0	0	0	0	0	0
1	0	0	3	3	3	3
2	0	0	3	4	4	7
3	0	0	3	4	5	7
4	0	0	3	4	5	7

Picture: 9.29

And the final answer is 7.

Question 9.14: Modify solution of Example 9.9 to also print the items that are picked to maximize the value.

Longest Palindromic Subsequence

Example 9.10: A subsequence of a string is the sequence of characters in the same relative order as they appear in the original string. Subsequence is explained in Example 9.5.

Given a string, find the length of longest subsequence that is also a palindrome. For example, if the string if BBABCBCAB then its subsequence BABCBAB is the longest subsequence that it also a palindrome, so our answer, length of such longest subsequence is 7.

I suggest you to study example 9.5 before reading further because we will be making many references to that example.

Recursive Solution

Let X be the given string and N be the number of characters in X. We compare the first character with last character of the string. If they are same, then both these characters are part of the palindromic subsequence and we continue finding other characters in subsequence by removing the first and last character from the string.

If first character is not same as the last character, then we find the longest palindromic subsequence of first N-1 characters and last N-1 characters and return the maximum of these two values.

Below is the C language code for the above logic. Initial values of start and end are 0 and n-1 respectively. At any point, they hold the index of first and last element of subarray under consideration.

```
int lps(char *str, int start, int end){

   // Terminating conditions
   if(start>end)
      return 0;
   if(start == end)
      return 1;
   // first and last char are same
   if (str[start] == str[end])
      return lps (str, start+1, end-1) + 2;
   else
      return getMax(lps(str, start, end-1),
             lps(str, start+1, end));
}
```

Code: 9.20

The above code is taking exponential time in the worst case, $O(2^n)$ to be precise. The worst case comes when LPS is of length 1 and first and last characters are never same.

Clearly, we are solving subproblems multiple times and Code 9.20 can be memoized using a table of size N*N, where cell (i,j) stores the LPS of substring starting from i^{th} character to j^{th} character. It is very similar to the memoized solution of example 9.5.

Dynamic Programming Solution

In DP solution, we use the logic discussed in recursion and populate the table, starting from top-left.

```
int lps(char *str, int n){
  if(str == NULL || *str == '\0')
   return 0;

  int table[n][n];

  // Single char str is palindrom of length 1
  // therefore initializing with 1
  for(int i = 0; i < n; i++)
   table[i][i] = 1;
  for(int k=2; k<=n; k++)
  {
    for(int i=0; i<n-k+1; i++)
    {
      int j = i+k-1;
      if(str[i] == str[j] && k == 2)
       table[i][j] = 2;
      else if(str[i] == str[j])
       table[i][j] = table[i+1][j-1] + 2;
      else
       table[i][j] = getMax (table[i][j-1],
                            table[i+1][j]);
    }
  }
  return table[0][n-1];

}
```

Code: 9.21

Note that, lower diagonal values of the table are useless and are not filled in the process, you may want to talk about use of sparse arrays (see footnote 14) in the interview.

Code 9.21 takes $O(n^2)$ time in the worst case which is an improvement over the exponential time recursive solution.

Question 9.15: Modify the above code to also print the longest palindromic sub sequence.

Dropping Eggs Puzzle

Example 9.11: We have two identical eggs and access to a 100 floor building.

We do not know how strong the eggs are. Eggs can be really strong and may not break even when dropped from 100th floor or they may be fragile and break if dropped from first floor itself.

We want to find out the highest floor from where eggs can be dropped without breaking it. In the process, we are allowed to break both the eggs.

Question is, at least how many times do we need to drop, to find the answer (highest floor from where eggs start breaking)?

It looks more like a puzzle than a DP question. Most puzzles asked in coding interviews have their solutions in some computer science concepts. That's why puzzles are asked in interviews of companies like Microsoft and Adobe.

Below we have discussed some of the solutions that you may come up during the interview starting from least optimal to most optimal. Interviews are not interrogation, they are discussions where the interviewer want to understand the interviewee more than selecting or rejecting him. It is a good idea to discuss more than one solutions during the interview

a) Linear Solution

- Start from the first floor, and keep moving one floor up at a time. From each floor drop the egg and see if it breaks.

- If the egg breaks at the kth floor, then answer is k.

Number of Drops required in the worst case: 100. *Note that this is the only way to solve the puzzle if we have one egg.* Think of it like the linear search in an array, where we traverse the array linearly in forward direction.

b) Absolute Binary Solution

In this solution we apply the logic of Binary search on the first egg and linear search on the second egg. In this solution we divide the interval of 100 floors in 2 equal halves and follow the following algorithm:

```
Drop the egg from 50'th floor
  IF Egg breaks
    Try with the 2nd egg starting from 1'st floor
    till 50th in a linear way.
  IF Egg does not break.
    Drop the egg from the 75th floor.
And so on...
```

Number of drops required in the worst case is 50.

c) Fixed Interval Approach

In the above approach we are always dividing the floors in two halves equal (intervals) for the first egg. The problem is that for second egg we have to move linearly. We do not get the $O(\lg(n))$ solution as in the case of Binary search because the binary-ness is only on the first egg and not on the complete solution (second egg is still linear).

In this approach we try to look for other intervals sizes (and not just half of the total). For example, what if we divide the total floors (100) in 4 equal intervals, ending at floor numbers, 25, 50, 75 and 100. The first egg is dropped from floor-25, then floor-50, then floor-75 and then floor-100. If it breaks on dropping from, say, floor-50, then the second egg is dropped linearly from floor-26 to floor-49.

We can pick any number of intervals. If we divide the floors in a way that each interval is of size k each, then the logic we are following is as follows:

```
curFloor = k
WHILE (curFloor <=100)
  Drop first egg from curFloor
  IF it breaks
    Drop second Egg starting from (curFloor-k+1)th
    floor till (curFloor-1) to get the answer.
  ELSE
    curFloor = curFloor + k
```

If we take k=25 (4 intervals), then minimum number of drops in the worst case are 28. But we do not know if it is the best answer. Table 9.2 shows the minimum number of drops required in the worst case for different intervals.

As seen, the minimum number of drops in the worst case decreases when we increase the interval. But after a particulat point (after 13 inervals), the minimum number of drops in the worst case starts increasing. So, if we follow this approach, then the minimum number of drops required in worst case is 19.

Interval	Num. of Drops	Interval	Num. of Drops
1	100	9	19
2	51	10	19
3	35	11	19
4	28	12	19
5	24	13	19
6	21	14	20
7	19	15	20
8	19	16	21

Table: 9.2

Minimum drops required is: 19 (For Interval $8, 9, 10, 11, 12$ & 13)

d) Variable Interval Approach

In previous approach, the size of interval for the first egg was fixed. In this case we are not using the same interval size every time.

Let x be the total number of drops required to find the correct floor number in optimal solution. If first egg breaks when it is dropped for the first time, then we have $x-1$ drops left for the second egg. Now second egg is dropped linearly, so the floor from which first egg was dropped must have been floor-x (so that there are $x-1$ floors from start till that point).

If the first egg does not break on its first drop, then we drop it again from, say, floor p. Let us assume that it breaks on the second drop. Now, 2 drops are used by the first egg, so $x-2$ drops are left for the second egg (because total number of drops are x). It means, first egg is dropped from a distance of $x-1$ after x (first interval). Second interval is of size $x-1$. And so on.

The last interval size is just 1. Sum of size of all the intervals must become greater than, or equal to 100, the total number of floors. The mathematical equation for this is

```
x + (x-1) + (x-2) + ... + (1) >= 100
```

Solving the equation for x, we get

```
x = 14
```

Hence, the total number of drops required = 14. This is the most optimal answer.

i.e drop the first egg from following floors until it breaks: `14, 27 (14+13), 39 (14+13+12), 50(14+13+12+11), 60, 69, 77, 84, 90, 95, 99, 100...`

If it breaks at any point, the second egg is dropped linearly from 1+ the previous floor from where the first egg was dropped.

Droping Eggs as DP Problem

Let us generalize the problem and say that we have n floors and x eggs. If we drop an egg from p^{th} floor, either the egg breaks or it does not break.

- If the egg breaks, then the floor that we are searching for is before floor-p, so we need to check for p-1 floors with remaining x-1 eggs.

- If the egg does not break, then the floor that we are searching for is after floor-p, so we need to check for n-p floors with x eggs.

The value that is maximum of the above two is our answer. We do so for all the floors, and return the minimum value. The logic is as follows:

```
int dropngEggs(int numFloors, int numEggs){
  // 0 Floor-0 drop needed. 1 floor-1 drop needed
  // Or if only 1 egg then drops = numFloors
  if(numFloors == 1 || numFloors == 0 || numEggs == 1)
    return numFloors;

  int min = INT_MAX;

  // droppings from 1st to last floor and return
  // minimum of these values plus 1.
  for (int p = 1; p <= numFloors; p++)
```

```
{
    int temp = getMax(dropngEggs(p-1, numEggs),
                dropngEggs (numFloors-p, numEggs));
    if (temp < min)
      min = temp;
}

return min + 1;
}
```

Code: 9.22

So there exist an optimal substructure property. If we draw the function call diagram we can see that subproblems are also overlapping. This makes the dropping eggs puzzle a fit case for dynamic programming.

We have practiced so many questions. Can you try solving it on your own ? A good problem to ponder is the best gift any teacher can give. Consider this a gift from our side ☺.

Made in the USA
Middletown, DE
22 December 2017